THE STATECRAFT
OF MACHIAVELLI

BY

H. BUTTERFIELD, M.A.
Master of Peterhouse, Cambridge

LONDON
G. BELL AND SONS LTD
1955

First published 1940
Reprinted 1955

PRINTED IN GREAT BRITAIN BY
BILLING AND SONS LIMITED GUILDFORD AND LONDON

I FEARE ME it had neede be a high point of pollicie, that should rob Master Machiavel of his
pollicie, especially if the surveier be himself an
straunger in the Italian territories.

GABRIEL HARVEY

CONTENTS

INTRODUCTION

LIVING from 1469 to 1527, Machiavelli saw what we may regard as the culmination of the Italian Renaissance. He was brought up while the Medici family were masters of Florence —while Lorenzo the Magnificent was gaining for the city a strategic position in Italian politics. He received a gentlemanly education, studied the classics, and learned at any rate to read and write in Latin, without gaining any particular reputation as a man of scholarship. His mentality is essentially that of his time and circle, and it is one of the purposes of the following essay to restore him to his context, from which he is too often and too easily divorced.

He was twenty-five when the first French invasion of Italy took place in 1494, and from this moment Florence entered upon a tumultuous history; for the Medici were driven out and a republic was proclaimed, and Savonarola became a predominant figure in the city for four years. Machiavelli's own chief political experience, however, coincides with the period of the second French invasion, 1499-1512. In 1498 he had been made Secretary of the Ten and besides writing thousands of official letters for this executive council, he was sent on numerous missions either to places under Florentine rule or to the governments of foreign states. It is to this period of the second French invasion that he principally refers for the topical examples which he discusses in *The Prince*. The expulsion of the French in 1512 and the return of the Medici to Florence put an end to these activities, however; and it was in exile that Machiavelli compiled those political treatises which it is our purpose to discuss.

No other treatises on the art of politics have so stirred the opinion of the world, provoking controversy in every generation. Bitter hatred and extravagant blame on the one hand have been met by patriotic enthusiasm and lyrical praise on the other. And some who have thought that Machiavelli could not have been so wicked as he appeared to be, have resorted to ingenious conjecture and recondite explanation. To some he has seemed the malevolent counsellor of tyrants; to others, the noble spokesman of a nation's liberties. To some he has seemed the most hard-hearted of realist politicians, while others have called him rather a philosopher who was more modern than the times would bear. On the Elizabethan stage he could be depicted as a professional inventor of stratagems and crooked tricks—the teacher of ruses whether for rogues and misers or for baffled lovers; but much ingenuity has been expended on the other hand in order to show why the Elizabethan dramatists should have been so wildly wrong. In the following essay an attempt has been made to study what Machiavelli himself had to say about his purpose and his science of statecraft; from which it may appear that he for his part would not always have ratified the interpretations which have been put upon him by his friends; and that the Anti-Machiavels and even the Elizabethan dramatists were not so wilfully wide of the mark as some writers have assumed.

Bolingbroke's view of Machiavelli chimes in with the view that is here presented; and in a certain sense the final chapter on "Machiavelli and Bolingbroke" serves to complete the argument or at least to provide a variation on the same theme. But, if Machiavelli has been unduly whitewashed (as though he were not so greatly a purveyor of stratagem), it might be said that Bolingbroke (in his capacity as the author of The *Patriot King*) has been unduly blackened, both Whigs and Tories having had their reasons for trying to disown him. If on the one hand he stood as a severe critic, he was also in a certain sense one of the principle English disciples of Machiavelli. And the study of the curious relationship between these writers not only helps to underline the comments made below on the author of *The Prince*, but is also one of the ways in which we may perhaps rectify the long misinterpretation of The *Patriot King*. That work must be the most famous English book written consciously as a counterpart (both a mirror and an answer) to *The Prince*. And, not because it is a great piece of literature, but because it has been such a fable amongst students of English history, it deserves to be re-examined in this connection.

I. THE FOUNDATIONS

MACHIAVELLI'S SCIENCE OF STATECRAFT

IN studying a writer like Machiavelli it is difficult to avoid seeing the man through the work of a long line of commentators, and imputing to him the theories which have been adduced at later times in order to expand or explain his thought. Nothing more greatly affects our interpretation of a book like *The Prince* or the *Discourses* than the expectations that we bring to the reading of it. We are easily induced to intercept the author's meaning by translating it into categories of our own, and if we have been led to focus our attention upon the wrong points we can easily convince ourselves that we have seen what we went to see. If we judge his work by the things which, though they are present, are merely incidental to its main design, or if we feel at liberty to impute to Machiavelli theories which to us are natural implications of statements that he made—though the author himself did not see the implications, or in any case did not feel it necessary to point them out—we are in a position to impose upon Machiavelli many of our own assumptions, conscious or unconscious, and we shall be greatly tempted to endow him with our modern mentality. It is important, therefore, that we should interpret Machiavelli in the light of his own aims and avowed intentions, seeking to know what his books signified to himself, and what precise changes he wished to make in the thought or the practice of his own day; and we are likely to confuse the issues if we even turn aside to discuss his place in history, or set out to examine his importance to the present day, and let our appreciation of his work be governed by this estimate. It is essential to discover where lay the peculiar genius of the man, and to find out what in real life was his dominating passion; and in particular to keep in mind the declared intention, rather than the historical consequences, of his political thought.

The purpose of Machiavelli's teaching has been often stated, though one might say that it has not always been kept in mind. Villari has said with truth that "the real aim of his researches and his science was the demonstration of precepts relating to political action." The essence of his teaching was the promotion of a more scientific statecraft and he made it clear that he wrote his books in order to produce an actual change in the practice of his day. He had a low opinion of the manner in which policy was conducted by his Italian contemporaries. He criticized particularly the princes who were ruling in Italy—and in western Europe—at the time. Since he had a very high opinion of his own capacity and knowledge his was a discontent that would feed upon itself during his compulsory exile from political life. And his contempt for the statecraft of his generation was justified in his eyes by the wretched condition of Italy. Many of the disasters which the world had been content to attribute to misfortune he looked upon as the result of improvidence and misrule. He wrote for an Italy which had been astounded by the facile conquests of the French in that first invasion of 1494; which had been repeatedly devastated since, and was becoming the chosen arena and the coveted prize of foreign nations. Not only Italy but every single state in the peninsula was endangered by the political instability that had ensued. And the tragedies gave an opening to a man who might claim to possess a new science of statecraft. Perhaps Machiavelli found it easy to underestimate the part played by historical circumstances in these disasters.

> Those of our princes who held their states for many years must not blame fortune for the eventual loss of them, but must put it down to their own indolence,

he wrote. The strength of his feeling on this point gave a bias to his discussion of the whole question of fortune.

Though it was his view that human beings can co-operate with fortune but not resist her—"can follow the order of her designs but can never hope to defeat them altogether"—it was the repeated claim of Machiavelli, and it was one of his argu-

ments on behalf of his science of statecraft, that a
certain region of historical event which contemporaries were content to accept as the province of
chance, could be brought under human control by
systematic and self-conscious statesmanship. He
protested against the view that men cannot change
events; he complained of those people who "allow
things to be governed by chance"; fortune, he said,

> shows her power where no resistance has been
> organized against her, and directs her attack
> upon those places where no embankments or
> barriers have been made to hold her back.

He asserted that unwise princes were "exposed to
sudden revolutions of fortune." He claimed in one
place that "those who carefully follow [these max-
ims] will find that they have much less need for the
assistance of fortune than others who fail to do so."
He showed that those new princes who "owed less
to fortune were more successful in maintaining
their power"; and that the "most excellent" of
them "owed nothing to chance save their opportunity." It is typical of his attitude to the whole subject that he could argue that the possession of dis-
ciplined troops tended to produce that very "good
luck" to which people liked to attribute their happiness or success; "but if a state is disarmed and
leaves itself entirely to the caprice of fortune it is
helpless before every change of the wind." Altogether he showed a special interest in that region

where human foresight or self-assertion could steal a victory over time and chance. It is not strange therefore that in a certain aspect his new statecraft was regarded as an insurance against the future. And—since most of these discussions have reference to the downfall of Italy, and particularly the invasion of 1494—it was an insurance against the very kind of "misfortune" of which the Italians of the time seemed so ready to complain.

It should be noted that Machiavelli's intention was not the study or the creation of that particular science which we to-day call political science; and it is important that we should come to his work as historians, not as theorists who hanker after synthesis. The science which he is regarded as having invented has indeed no point save in its detail. It was always a particular policy or expedient that he was commending for adoption by the practical statesman; or it was an element conditioning political action that he was subjecting to analysis. His teaching is a collection of concrete maxims—warnings and injunctions in regard to certain points of policy, rules of conduct for specified emergencies, and expositions of tactical moves. He gives us the principles to observe if we wish to retain a foreign conquest or to found a new state that is intended for aggrandizement; the conduct to pursue when our neighbours are at war, or when a subject is becoming dangerous, or when institutions are to be altered; the ruses to be employed when besieging a city, or dealing with conspirators, or handling a refractory people.

That this science of statecraft existed as a collection of maxims in Machiavelli's own mind can be seen by a collation of his various writings. In his official correspondence and in his private letters, when he was commenting on the past in his historical writing or trying to prophesy what a certain monarch would do in the future—whenever he had to apply a criterion to events or wished to pass judgement upon political action—Machiavelli would continually draw upon these maxims which seem to have existed in his mind as a basis of reference. The same maxims recur in *The Prince*, the *Discourses*, the *History of Florence*, and the private letters; the statecraft in all these writings is continuous and the exposition is of the same texture throughout; our judgement of Machiavelli and his science is independent of that special pleading which is so often done on behalf of *The Prince*.

It has been said that the first dawnings of this science of statecraft "were visible in the epistles and reports of ambassadors and statesmen." Through Machiavelli the concrete political discussions of a diplomatic dispatch or a ministerial paper were turned into the accumulated wisdom of the printed book and organized into a new science. He himself had written these ambassadorial reports and secretarial papers when he was in the service of the republic of Florence. When he lost his official position, even when he was removed from authentic sources of information, he remained at heart—what he so desired to become again in reality—a professional adviser on political questions and one whose skill was the admiration of his friends. He said that because he was "incapable of talking of silk and wool or profit and loss" he must go on discussing matters of government or be silent; and his private letters in this period of exile read like official diplomatic reports. On one occasion he was asked to advise the Papacy on a point of policy and it was thought that this exhibition of his powers would lead to his restoration to political life. At another time—at the moment when the Medici family had been restored in Florence in 1512—he wrote to members of the family, offering them political advice; and what he had to say had reference to the special problems which a new prince had to face in territory recently acquired. From this to the writing of *The Prince*—essentially a treatise on new principalities—and the dedication of the book to another Medici ruler with the same object of securing an official appointment, is only a very short transition; for Machiavelli in compulsory retirement wanted to give an exhibition of his skill, tended to be critical of politicians in action, and had a desperate desire to regain an influence in public affairs. In this way the new science of statecraft developed out of ministerial correspondence, and sprang more or less directly from the practical world; and Machiavelli did not invent statecraft itself, and was not the first to put concrete political advice into writing; he is important because during his exile he accumulated it into a book. We must not say, therefore, that he took hold of political theory and transported it from speculative realms to a region of empirical observation. The subject of his labour was the science of statecraft, and, as we shall see, he made this science more theoretical than before, attaching it to certain dogmas that belonged to the schools. For along with the practical politician there was in Machiavelli something of the doctrinaire. The acutest of his contemporary critics, Guicciardini, objected to his work precisely on this score.

Machiavelli was original most of all in his claim that statecraft could be erected into a permanent science. One of his biographers has noted that he continually asserts: "and this must be held as a general rule." Guicciardini, who was a younger contemporary, always maintained that in politics no general rule holds good. He denied that practical wisdom could be embodied in a book and asserted that long experience and native discretion were the essential guides to political action. When Guicciardini wrote his maxims he repeatedly offered the following kind of warning:

Bear in mind what I said before about these maxims, how they are not always to be put into practice without discrimination; in some special cases they are not serviceable. And what these cases are is a matter that cannot be comprehended by any rule, neither is there any book which can teach them; but this is a thing which must be learned first from nature and then from experience.

Now it is evident, not only from the character of Machiavelli's maxims but also from the way in which he applied his precepts to contemporary problems, that he differed from Guicciardini in a certain rigidity and dogmatism. He presses his theses with urgency, says that the surest way to ruin a state is to contravene a certain principle, and announces that everything is easy if only this or that rule is obeyed. Sometimes he gives extravagant promises of success to those princes who will follow the precepts he has set down. It would seem that any prince who follows these maxims must succeed as Philip of Macedon had done. He can write: "It is vain therefore to think of ever retrieving Italian arms by any method save such as I have described"; or he can claim: "Whoever pursues this method in a city that is besieged will find it easy to defend the place." And when he says that above all things a prince ought to avoid incurring the general hatred of his subjects, he can add in a manner that is not unusual with him: "and how he is to do this I have explained in another place."

It will be seen later that some defect in Machiavelli produced a certain lack of subtlety in his feeling for the interplay of historical events. Student of chance and change, of all the processes of time, he yet had an imperfect sense of their perpetual mobility. Guicciardini would assert that it was wrong for a man to argue, as many do: "Either this will happen or that other thing will happen, and if this happens I will act in this way but if the other thing happens I will do this other way." He would speak of other factors intervening, further complications that no man could predict. He was intensely aware of the combination of chances which might arise to cheat our attempts at prophecy and to deflect our purposes. On shifting sands like these no science of statecraft could find a hold. Machiavelli did not overlook the place of fortune in the affairs of men—indeed he had reason to complain of it too often in the vicissitudes of his own career— but as we have seen he was inclined to emphasize the view that men could insure themselves against the caprice of time and chance. He does in fact argue, if this happens, you must act in this way, but if the other thing happens you must do this other way; and his zeal in the discussion of alternative cases only helps to give the impression that he is providing for all eventualities. It is not strange therefore that even when Guicciardini and Machiavelli are in general agreement on a certain point of policy—as in the case of the thesis that it is wrong to remain neutral when neighbours are at war—it is Machiavelli who persistently presses the maxim in an absolute form; while Guicciardini makes reservations and allows for the unforeseeable nature of circumstances. So Machiavelli was able to create a science of politics in the sense of a body of rules upon which governments should act and should absolutely rely. Guicciardini on the contrary makes policy a perpetual course of improvization. He represents the view that government is not a science but an art.

MACHIAVELLI'S HISTORICAL METHOD

IF the new science of statecraft had its origin, on the one hand, in the dispatches and state papers of government servants, it is connected also, on another side, with the development of historical study and the rise of the Florentine school of historians. If there are passages in Machiavelli's letters which might have been part of his treatises on politics, there are also passages in his *History of Florence* which might have occurred in either. It was a time when the writers of history were often also administrators or diplomatists versed in government and public affairs; and the historians of this period in Florence seemed to show a special interest in the events that were nearly contemporary. They brought their practical experience and their love of political discussion into their historical inquiries—trying to seize upon faults in policy, or to explain a political decision or a military defeat. Machiavelli's criticism in *The Prince* of the conduct of Louis XII during the second French invasion, can be paralleled by Guicciardini's comments, scattered more diffusely in his narrative of the wars. There was a further reason why these writers were so able to regard recent events in a light that was at the same time practical and historical. It is surprising to what an extent the Italians of these days felt that their world had been shaken and cut in two by the invasion of 1494. Guicciardini, setting out in his history to give "an account of the troubles in Italy together with the causes from which so many evils were derived," opened his narrative with the words:

> It is certain that, for above a thousand years— since the Roman Empire, weakened by a change in her ancient institutions, began to decline from the height of grandeur to which amazing virtue and good fortune had helped to bring her—Italy had at no time enjoyed a state of such complete prosperity and repose, as in the year 1490, and some time before and after.

The consciousness that the year 1494 had opened the gates to disasters which had tormented Italy ever since, was a great incentive to historical inquiry and political analysis in other people besides Machiavelli; and the country seemed moved, as we were moved after the War of 1914, to enter upon a more intensive self-examination.

But Machiavelli distinguished himself by claiming that in the study of history one could discover not only the causes but also the cure of the ills of the time. Where he was peculiar, where he provoked the criticism of Guicciardini, and where he earnestly desired to convert the Italians of his day, was in his attitude to historical study—his peculiar views concerning the utility of history. His position was based upon the combination of certain theories, each of which, taken separately, was perhaps not uncommon in sixteenth-century Italy—theories which Guicciardini himself held in a certain manner and even would express in very similar terms; though Guicciardini did not apprehend them with the same rigidity, or accept them in the same way as the basis of further inference—did not admit that a science of statecraft could be founded on them or that Machiavelli was justified in the combination that he made of these views. The theories in question were first of all a doctrine of "imitation," which conditioned Machiavelli's attitude to the great men of the past; secondly an important thesis concerning historical recurrence, one that affected therefore the problem of the deduction of general laws from historical data; and thirdly a conviction of the superiority of the ancient world as a guide to human behaviour in the present. These three aspects of Machiavelli's thought represent what perhaps were the most typical features in Renaissance theory on the subject of the past. But in Machiavelli they acquired new power by their combination—reinforcing one another by their mutual interactions. They gave, indeed, a peculiar shape to his doctrine concerning the utility of history.

The doctrine of imitation, applied particularly

to the example of great men, appears on numerous occasions and can be found in various passages of *The Prince*. It can be seen in the dedication of this book and also in the address in the final chapter. The general thesis is most clearly stated in Chapter VI:

> Nobody must be surprised if in my discussion of new principalities ... I make reference to very imposing examples; for as men nearly always follow the path traced by others and proceed in their actions by imitation—though they cannot quite keep to the path or reach the full merits of those whom they imitate—a prudent man ought always to walk in the path traced out by great men and imitate those who are most excellent, so that if he does not attain their prowess he may at least achieve something of the flavour of it.

The actual workings of this principle are apparent in some such passages as the following, which is from the *Discourses on Livy*:

> Those who wish to learn the method to adopt for the achievement of this end, need not take any more trouble than to put before their eyes the lives of good men, such as Timoleon the Corinthian, Aratus the Sicyonian, and the like; in whose lives they will see so much mutual confidence and satisfaction existing between the people governing and

the people governed, that they will desire to imitate the conduct of these men, which they will find to be an easy matter.

Disc. III 5.

Constantly we meet sentences like the following, from the *Art of War*:

If then our princes would read and duly consider the lives and fortunes of these great men, one would think it impossible that they should not alter their conduct.

The second of Machiavelli's theses was based on the view that human nature is unchanging throughout the ages. Human passions, being constant, move men at all periods to the same kinds of action, driving the story to the same crises and conjunctures; so that history tends to fall into repeating patterns, instead of progressing to an unforeseeable future that is pregnant with hidden shapes. In other words, the course of history does not generate new things, and with all its host of accidents and incidents, the world throughout the centuries remains essentially the same; events occur in only a limited number of combinations; and historical situations perpetually repeat themselves, dissolving for a season but then re-forming after the ancient pattern. On this view of history change is kaleidoscopic—there is reshuffling and recombination but no transformation of the constituent

parts; historical change is not regarded as the process of an evolutionary development in which each
stage of the story means the attainment of something new. Machiavelli holds this view of historical
recurrence with a certain rigidity; he is not content
(as we perhaps should be) to say that, at certain
periods of the past, situations and events provided
mere analogies with things that we know in the
present. Guicciardini, as we might expect, showed
the greater elasticity in this matter, though stating
the doctrine of historical recurrence in terms very
similar to those of Machiavelli himself. Guicciardini, indeed, stressed a different aspect of the topic,
insisting, as we have already seen, upon the com-
plexity of historical change. He notes that every
episode involves factors which make it not quite
like any historical parallels that can be adduced.
He emphasizes the view that each historical episode
is unique in some way; each must be treated therefore as a special case. So, while Guicciardini says
that too much must not be made of historical examples, Machiavelli on the other hand uses the
doctrine of historical recurrence with remarkable
effect. It enables him to go to history for the discovery of general rules and political precepts, and
he can regard these as possessing universal validity,
since they have reference to conjunctures that are
always likely to recur.

His view can be illustrated from a passage which
is taken from the *Discourses*:

Whoever considers things present and things past will easily understand how the same appetites and humours are and always have been incident to all states and people, so that by diligently examining the course of former ages it is an easy matter for men to foresee what is going to happen in any commonwealth, and not only to provide such remedies against future evils as their predecessors did, but (if there be no precedent) to strike out new ones on the basis of the existing analogies. But since considerations of this kind are too often neglected or little understood, or are beyond the knowledge of those men who govern states, it comes to pass that the same evils and inconveniences take place in all ages of history.

Disc. I 39.

Towards the close of the same work there is an even stronger statement of the thesis:

Wise men say (and perhaps not unjustly) that in order to form an impression of what is yet to come, we ought to consider what is already passed; for there is nothing in this world at present, or at any other time, but has and will have its counterpart in antiquity; which happens because these things are operated by human beings who, having the same passions in all ages, must necessarily behave uniformly in similar situations. *Disc. III* 43.

Accepting the fact that men are alike and that they tend to imitate one another, Machiavelli asks that this imitation shall become conscious and shall be an imitation of the best. Accepting the fact that events are for ever repeating themselves, he insists that we shall take advantage of it, read history, and learn the best that has been done in previous cycles. He required only one further stage of reasoning to bring his views to that point of rigidity which gives the lessons of history their greatest simplification; and that was the addition of the final thesis that there was one particular period of history so noteworthy in its success and happiness— one particular cycle which had so long cheated the inevitable process towards corruption—that the modern world could do nothing better than accept it as the pattern for its own conduct, not merely seeking to recapture its prevailing spirit, but copying its methods in the concrete, piece by piece. It was avowedly upon the imitation of antiquity— though an antiquity interpreted by him, whether he knew it or not, in the light of contemporary Italian situations and needs—that he based his new science of politics and took up a particular position in which he seems to have regarded himself as standing against the world.

His attitude towards his science of statecraft is explained in the place where we should most expect to find the exposition of his fundamental conception—in the Introduction to Book I of the *Dis-*

courses, which represented his most elaborate political work. It is here that he makes his claim to originality and if his views are considered in the light of the historical principles that have just been set forward, it will be seen why his friend Nardi, on hearing readings from the *Discourses*, declared that the work was "of new argument, never attempted by any other man, so far as I know." It will be seen why Machiavelli himself, in the Dedicatory Letter to the *Discourses*, could write:

> Although, owing to the envious nature of men, it is always as dangerous to discover new orderings and ways as to explore unknown lands and seas—for human beings are always more ready to blame than to praise the actions of their fellows—nevertheless . . . I have resolved to enter upon a path that has not yet been trodden by human foot.

The Introduction makes reference to the veneration with which classical works of art are regarded by Machiavelli's contemporaries—"how often it happens (to omit other instances) that an immense price is given by the curious for a fragment of an old statue that will serve as an adornment for a cabinet or a model for artists"; and Machiavelli comments on the trouble which artists are willing to take in order to come up to the standard of classical works which they have adopted as their pattern. He goes on to show how lawyers take their precepts and doctors borrow their remedies from the practitioners of the ancient world; "in civil differences, as well as in the various maladies that are incident to mankind, we always have recourse to such decisions and prescriptions as have been handed down to us from our ancestors." Yet, he says, the "deeds of former kings, generals, citizens, 'Legislators' etc. are now rather admired than adopted for imitation":

In establishing a republic, in maintaining a state, in governing a kingdom, in organizing an army and conducting a war, in administering a subject people, in extending an empire, there is neither prince nor republic, nor general nor citizen who makes reference to the precedents in antiquity. . . The cause of this is the lack of a true understanding of history—the failure to take from history that significance and appreciate that wisdom which it contains. Those who read it and delight to hear the varieties of incident which it narrates, do so without dreaming of taking examples for imitation. . . Desiring however to induce men to forsake this error I have thought it necessary to write a commentary upon those books of Titus Livius which have been spared us by the malevolence of time. I shall refer to both ancient and modern affairs in order that these books may be better under-

35

stood; so that those who read these Discourses may reap that advantage which ought to be their object when they come to the study of history.

Ten years before he had begun writing his books, Machiavelli had stated the whole thesis in similar terms in a small treatise on the *Method of dealing with the rebels of the Val di Chiana*. Here he writes:

> I have heard it said that history is the master of our actions and especially of the policy of princes; and the world was always inclined to sameness, inhabited as it is by men who in all ages have the same passions. Always there were the men who served and the men who had command; men who gladly served and men who served with a bad will. . . So, if it is true that history is the master of our actions, it would have been useful if the men who had to chastise and administer the district of Val-dichiana had taken example from those who were masters of the world and had imitated their actions, especially in a case in which there was a clear precedent concerning the conduct to pursue.

Earlier than this, on 21st November 1500, he had shown that he intended this teaching to be followed by practical statesmen; for commenting on Louis XII's invasion of Italy, he had said: "His

Majesty ought to follow the methods of those who in past times have wished to possess a foreign province": and he had put forward some of the maxims which were to be learned from history—maxims later elaborated in *The Prince* and further expanded in the *Discourses*. And according to this latter work, where the source of the maxims is more clearly revealed, it is evident that, on Machiavelli's view, Louis XII, when he desired conquests in Italy, ought to have "got up the subject" of foreign conquest by historical study and followed the examples of the ancient Romans.

It is a mistake to water down the meaning of the very passage in which Machiavelli states—as indeed on many other occasions—the fundamental point of his new science. It is wrong to imagine that he was merely pleading for the growth of wisdom, the widening of experience which may come to any man from historical study; or to think that he would have been satisfied to see his contemporaries vaguely inspired with the idea of conducting themselves like Romans. The analogies that he makes—the artist copying classical models, the physician taking his prescriptions, the lawyer following ancient laws—are very striking; and to these may be added the case of the art of war where Machiavelli's principle of direct imitation is most marked. His attitude to history and antiquity implied in him a preoccupation with concrete cases and practical instances—an emphasis upon history as a storehouse of examples rather than a field of experience in a more elastic sense of the words. And this is in keeping with many of his habitual statements—his very vocabulary and his *clichés*—when he is speaking of the lessons of the past. His doctrine of imitation does in fact mean the imitation of definite specimens of successful policy, with a particular stress on the actions of great men and on the examples of antiquity. Speaking roughly and stating the case perhaps at its crudest, we may say that the position he takes up rests on the view that if a certain expedient has proved successful in some conjuncture in the past, the trick ought not to be forgotten in a world in which historical situations are being constantly repeated. Studying history in examples, Machiavelli draws lessons from striking incidents, and catches the very tones of the schoolteacher who rounds off the story with a moral—saying perpetually: "From this short narrative we may observe . . ."; "It behoves all princes, therefore"; "whoever reads this passage will see how necessary it is"—and then will follow some political maxim. Guicciardini, therefore, is really attacking the view of Machiavelli when he urges that it is not useful to make deductions from particular examples, and says that a very small modification of circumstances makes the historical precedent inapplicable. History does not quite repeat itself, he maintains, and every example in history has features which make it a special case.

Machiavelli, then, hoped by the study of antiquity to discover practical precepts and definite rules of political action, doing this specifically, as physicians and lawyers were in the habit of doing when they needed fresh remedies or principles of law. If he had intended anything short of this he would hardly have had to complain of the indifference of his contemporaries in Renaissance Italy to the examples of ancient Rome. Nor would Guicciardini have criticized his position—sharing, as he did, the general admiration for the Roman practice, but repudiating the idea that sixteenth-century statesmen should attempt to copy it in detail.

> How greatly do those men deceive themselves who at every point quote the example of the Romans [said Guicciardini]. It would be necessary to have a state under the same conditions as theirs, before one could take them as the model for political action.

Imitating the Romans, he argued, was only to be compared with the spectacle of the ass trying to run in a horse race. In military matters he ridiculed Machiavelli's curious disparagement of fire-arms —merely because the Romans did not make war with gunpowder! And while Machiavelli complained of those who questioned the authority of Livy, as though he were the inventor of "idle stories," Guicciardini expressed a certain scepticism not only concerning Livy but also on the subject of historians in general. If we can take the appeal to the classical world as a parallel to the Protestant regard for the authority of the Bible, Guicciardini represents the free or modernist view —and indeed it is not to be considered that any man of those days would have rejected the authority of the ancients altogether—but Machiavelli is the 'fundamentalist', the devotee of 'verbal inspiration,' more slavish than his political contemporaries in his reverence for the statecraft of the ancient world.

Upon this topic he is most militant in his writings, most conscious that he diverges from the majority of his contemporaries. And not only does he despise the statecraft of his epoch, but repeatedly he shows that the seat of their error lies precisely here. In the Preface to the second book of the *Discourses* he sets out to defend himself against the criticism that he is one of the men who blindly praise the ancients and blindly disparage the present time.

I do not know if I deserve to be numbered amongst those who deceive themselves [he writes] when in my discourses I praise the antique Roman times so much, while condemning the contemporary age. And, in truth, if the virtue which then prevailed and the vice which reigns to-day were not more clear than the sun, I should proceed in a more restrained manner in order to prevent myself from falling into that kind of self-deception... But since the thing is so manifest that every person with eyes can see it, I shall let myself go and make no bones about what I believe on the subject of the past and the present; so that the minds of the young who may read my writings, may shun the latter and prepare to imitate the former, whenever fortune shall give them the opportunity.

II. MACHIAVELLI AND THE RENAISSANCE

THE CULT OF ANTIQUITY

THE thought of the Renaissance reaches at certain points an extraordinary emancipation from religious authority and medieval prepossessions; but it has curious features which seem to savour now of the occult and now of the archaic, and even when it is irreligious we must not be too ready to call it modern. To free oneself from the tyranny of the past or from the dominion of the written and spoken word is never easy. Even to-day it requires a great exertion, a genuine effort of will, if not always actual originality of mind. And the men of the Renaissance we must remember, the humanists in particular, did not wish to be so emancipated. To consult the classics on all matters, to imitate the ancient world, was indeed for them the great adventure—the source and secret of that intellectual exhilaration which was the glory of the Italy of this time. The Protestants, who pushed their reverence for the ancient Scriptures to that extreme which came to be described as Bibliolatry; the followers of Aristotle who, for over a century after this, resisted novel theories concerning the physical structure of the universe; the medical students who now despised medieval science and turned the Arabians into a by-word, because they had found a more direct route to ancient Greece; the humanists who so deprecated the use of the vernacular that they checked the brilliant course of Italian literature and made imitative Latin verses the fashion, and who attempted, by copying Cicero, to turn Latin into a dead language—the Latin which for centuries had been rough and alive, a handy means of international communication for scholars—all these are only extreme examples of what was in fact a general adoration of antiquity.

In their devotion to the ancient culture the men of the Renaissance were most like their medieval predecessors. Perhaps it is true to say that their subservience to the classics was even more complete. We must note that the idea of a progressive development taking place in the course of centuries— the world moving forward to an unimagined future, to wider horizons and opening vistas—is a modern one. The idea of history as an ascending process was not part of the equipment of a Renaissance mind. In any case such a view of history could not congenially combine with current assumptions concerning the tendency of all composite bodies to disintegrate. The self-conscious development of the sciences in the seventeenth century; the rising importance of a knowledge that grows by sheer accumulation and deepens as one man takes up the researches of his predecessors; the technical progress that comes to be achieved in finance and industry and organization; the cumu-

lative results of inventions, discoveries, better com-
munications, speedier interchange of thought—
these are the factors that have helped men to believe in a future big with the promise of better
things. It was not until the seventeenth century that
the world finally faced the problem of the Ancients
versus the Moderns. And perhaps we owe the currency of the idea of progress chiefly to the grand
hopefulness and complacency of the French 'philo-
sophic' movement. We to-day can see the results of
a portentous speeding-up of those processes which
cause mutation in society. Perhaps life and the
world, and the general appearance of the country-
side, change more quickly now in one generation
than at one time they changed in the course of
many centuries. It is more easy now than in the
more static world of the sixteenth century to believe
that apart from the ups and downs of cities and
states, apart from variations in mere clothing and
custom, there is process in history, something more
than cycle and succession, something more than
Rome replacing Greece. Machiavelli, like his contemporaries, naturally assumed that apart from
superficial variations of an external character, the
world throughout the ages remains substantially
the same. In the Preface to Book II of the *Discourses* he writes:

And when I meditate upon the workings of
these matters, I come to the conclusion that

the world always remains in very much the same condition. The good and the bad balance one another, but each varies from region to region, as anybody can see who pays attention to the kingdoms of antiquity; for though these might have differed in their customs, the world as a whole continued its course in much the same way. The only difference was that, whereas at one time this virtue was assembled in Assyria, it passed to Media, then to Persia, and then to Italy and Rome. And if since the Roman Empire there has been no enduring empire, and no place in which all the virtue was assembled at one time, that virtue is nevertheless scattered about amongst the many nations [not including the Italy of the Renaissance, we may note] in which life is meritoriously carried on.

Further than this, having no principle of progress, these men possessed and were bound to possess, the converse conception which regards history as normally a process of decline. According to the current belief, it was in the nature of compound bodies to disintegrate; and human societies and institutions were compound bodies in this sense. It is apparent in the work of Machiavelli—in the early part of the *Discourses*, for example—and in the thought of the age, that the ascent of states, the rise to prosperity and virtue, was regarded as something of a miracle, a wonderful over-riding of the normal working of things in nature; on the other hand decline was in the ordinary processes of time, only to be checked by unsleeping vigilance and extraordinary endeavour. A great law-giver, a mighty act of volition, a stroke of fine fortune, might bring a state to a condition of greatness and power; by a grand intervention—a cataclysmic event —a decadent people might be restored to a condition of soundness and of public morality; but a degenerate people, ordinarily speaking, could not recover themselves again (any more than water could rise above its own level), as Machiavelli pointed out; and, even when greatness had been achieved, it was held that corruption soon set in, by an automatic process, if vigilance was relaxed for a moment and extraordinary energy was not continuously displayed.

So the men of the Renaissance believed in a closed culture, and did not imagine that civilization could be indefinitely expanding—continually producing new things. The boundaries of that culture had been reached in ancient Greece and Rome, and men could only revolve ancient things anew, could only hope to travel over the same ground and win the old truths back again, could only dream of equalling perhaps the achievements and the prowess of the ancient days. More strongly than the generations that preceded them they believed that since classical times the whole world had been wandering in darkness; and though when they said that wisdom lay in "antiquity," it might seem that they had in mind the prudence and the knowledge that come with the multitude of years, it did not occur to them to see that the world of Greece and Rome was on this view younger than theirs—that, as the centuries advance, mankind in fact gets older and wiser. It was a generation after the death of Machiavelli that Giordano Bruno in *La Cena de le Ceneri* thought it worth while to expose the current fallacy in regard to this matter:

If you properly understood what you were saying you would see that from your principle there follows a conclusion which is exactly the contrary to the one you have in mind: I mean that it is we who are older and who have a greater multitude of years than our predecessors; at any rate as regards certain topics, like the one with which we are dealing at the moment [the Copernican theory]. The judgement of Eudoxus who lived shortly after the rebirth of astronomy (if the renaissance did not actually take place through him) could not be so mature as that of Callippus, who lived thirty years after the death of Alexander the Great; and who, as year succeeded year, could add observation to observation. Hipparchus for the same reason must have known more than Callippus. . . More has been seen by Copernicus, almost in our day.

It is not too much to say that the thinkers of the Renaissance were undoubtedly right in the main general conclusion that they drew from their theory of history. From their point of view the classical world was the peak of civilization; and devotion to it had not yet become mere bondage for the scientific mind. Also, we may add that in many of their aspects the classics became, and long remained, one of the important constituents of the modern world. In any case English students should glance sympathetically even upon the prejudices of the Renaissance on the subject of the historical process; for these may be said to have become blended with our own fortunes and embedded in our political consciousness. When the Whigs emerged victorious in England towards the close of the seventeenth century, they did not stand out as the apostles of modernity and progress. Renaissance views on the processes of history were part of the make-up of their minds. The theory of decline which we are examining at the moment was part of the structure of their interpretation of history. Always the Golden Age would seem to have been behind them, if even occasionally one could only impute it to a dim and unspecified past. Always it was said that the Glorious Revolution "restored our constitution to its primitive vigour" and recovered the liberty that our ancestors had enjoyed. The Revolution indeed brought our government "back to its first principles" and reasserted the rightness of an ancient law. Furthermore, the Whigs who believed that liberty ever tends to decline unless men are constantly vigilant, that, if liberty is to be preserved in a new age, fresh laws and institutions must be devised to guard it against unforeseen dangers, that no laws can preserve liberty if the people themselves have become corrupted, saw the force of these maxims with special vividness because they were near to a view of history that stressed the tendency to decline. Into English Whiggism, in fact, passed the most benevolent of the maxims of Machiavelli himself; who had discussed the decay of liberty, the policies that would serve to arrest decline, and the whole problem of corruption in the state.

These ideas upon the classical world and the historical process are the background against which we must see the work of Machiavelli; and in the light of them it becomes the more remarkable that this man should have reproached his contemporaries for their indifference to the ancient world. In pursuing the cult of antiquity into the realm of statecraft and urging that imitation should be definite and detailed, he outstripped his generation; here he himself claimed to be unique and his contemporaries seem to have regarded him as such; and this we have seen was the very thing which he specified as the contribution that he had to make. Whereas the philosopher and scientist looked to ancient Greece, he, as a political teacher, put all his faith in republican Rome. The principal exposition of his statecraft is a commentary on Livy. His treatise on the *Art of War* is an essay on the imitation of the Romans. Perhaps the greatest effect of the isolated reading of *The Prince*, and the special notoriety that this book has enjoyed in so many generations, has been an underestimation of the strength of his devotion and the greatness of his debt to antiquity. For in *The Prince* his obligations to classical history and ancient writers are for the most part concealed; and the statecraft—though it is always the same statecraft—has been given a more topical bearing than in the other treatises. A generation ago a German writer, Ellinger, however, traced some of the classical borrowings in *The Prince* and many such borrowings are noted in Burd's edition. It will be seen below that Machiavelli's indebtedness to the Romans is not any less remarkable in this book than in the rest of his political writings.

In general Machiavelli's statements on the imitation of the Romans are remarkably specific, and unmistakable in their insistence:

> From all these considerations the true method appears to be the one which the Romans used, and it is all the more remarkable in that it has never been adopted by any other people before or since. . . We might add by way of conclusion that many other rules

which the Romans observed in conducting their affairs both at home and abroad are not only not imitated in these days but are treated with definite lack of consideration; some of them being looked upon as mere fables, others as impossible and others again as not appropriate or of no utility; and to this ignorant attitude we owe the fact that our country of late has been the prey of every invader who cared to come.

Disc. II 4.

In the sixth chapter of the first book of the *Discourses*, he shows that in founding a state it is better to follow the Romans and establish the state for purposes of aggrandizement and not merely for long duration. It had already been suggested in the preceding chapter that "if the state be designed to extend its dominion . . . the conduct of the Romans must be imitated in every particular."

Machiavelli's argument for the adoption of his maxims is the assertion that by following them the Romans achieved their success and renown. The question as to which form of government he preferred is an easy one to answer both from his own statements and by inference from the principles he puts forward. He did not admire ancient Rome because the Romans had a republic; he admired republican government because it was the form under which ancient Rome had achieved unex-

ampled greatness and power. He admired Switzerland, and feared her designs on Italy, and was once
reproved for suggesting that she would "do what
the ancient Romans had done"; and this was because from ancient Rome he had gained a high
opinion of what he called "armed republics" and
considered Switzerland to stand in this class. And
there is no contradiction when Machiavelli tells us
in one place that a mixed form of government—a
combination of monarchy, aristocracy, and democracy—is best; for he had learned from ancient
writers to consider republican Rome in this very
light, stressing the combination of consuls, senate,
and plebs. One might have inferred from Machiavelli's beliefs on the subject of history and fortune
that if a race like the Romans had existed as an example of happy achievement and public well-being,
he would have opposed the view which tended to
ascribe this success to good fortune and combinations of circumstances; he would have preferred to
attribute it to virtue and good policy which he
would enjoin future generations to copy. This is
what actually happens in the *Discourses* though
Machiavelli has to differ from both Plutarch and
Livy on the point.

His imitation of the ancients implied the acceptance of their precepts as well as their practice, and
in particular the acceptance of many of the
maxims or historical comments of ancient writers.
Those who like to think that he merely pretended

to possess the authority of ancient examples, which he did not use save as cover for policies of his own, cannot deny that he followed ancient precepts even in numerous cases where he did not pretend to be doing so at all. *The Prince* itself, which has such close relations with Machiavelli's period of active political service, contains a remarkable assortment of quotations, imitations, paraphrases, or variations of the teaching of antiquity. The very idea of the 'new prince' as the founder of a new state and a new condition of things is based upon classical writers; and the application of this idea to the special purpose of the amelioration of the condition of Italy has been ascribed to the influence of Xenophon's *Hiero*. This book, which Machiavelli had certainly read, and which he called by the title *De Tyrannide*, dealt with the situation and problems of a new prince who had gained power in a state that had hitherto been free; and it influenced *The Prince* in a number of details if not in the general lines of the theme. The dedication to *The Prince* opens with a passage which we are told is modelled upon Isocrates, and the final chapter exhorting the new prince to deliver Italy from the barbarians has resemblances to Isocrates' exhortation to Philip, though the direct connection has in this latter case been disputed. The dictum that the prince must imitate the fox and the lion; the recurring suggestion that conquests can be maintained if only the family of the dispossessed ruler is wiped out; the view that the prince can avoid hatred if he does not usurp the property and the women of his subjects; the claim that a prince should have no other aim or thought or preoccupation but war—all these and many others too numerous to mention have been shown to be close reproductions of the opinions of ancient writers.

Finally the very method by which Machiavelli proposed to discover statecraft from the examples of history, and all the principles upon which his "lessons of history" were based—the doctrine of imitation, the view that human nature is constant, the idea that history runs in cycles and that similar situations and problems recur—all are a heritage from the ancient world, a further proof of his discipleship. And I do not think we realize how often even when Machiavelli seems to be inductive, seems to be describing the contemporary world, he is really only making deductions from classical theses concerning human nature or the historical process (as may be seen in the letters translated on pages 116 to 121 below). We must not regard his statecraft in the first place as the result of observation of the contemporary world. It is rather Guicciardini who is the modern observer standing already in the clear light of day. Machiavelli is that other kind of person who can be so troublesome to the practising politician—the assured and insistent historian, the dogmatic disciple of the ancient ways. And he created his science of statecraft only

because he was less modern than Guicciardini—
entering more fully and with an almost medieval
rigidity into the Renaissance cult and imitation of
ancient Rome.

THE "RISE OF THE INDUCTIVE METHOD"

IN the light of what has been said in previous chapters we may now examine the place of Machiavelli in the transition which is often described as the "rise of the inductive method." By this is meant the modern insistence upon empirical data, the idea of grounding the sciences upon a firm basis of verifiable observations, the patient and assured promotion of knowledge by the collection, the collation, and the analysis of what we call facts. Those who imagine that the so-called inductive method sprang full-grown upon a world newly awakened from deep slumber in the Age of the Renaissance have a clear view of what they regard as its opposite, what they are ready to condemn as the medieval method. They have in mind first of all the adoption of scientific truths in virtue of some authority—on the strength of some ancient writer or some dictate of revealed religion. Or, on the other hand, they refer to the particular form of inquiry which seeks explanations of the universe by a long process of inference and deduction—which, raising too high a structure of reasoning upon too small a basis of verifiable facts, gives the whole argument a flimsy and airy appearance, as though the sciences were left floating far from contact with reality in a region of abstract thought.

The veneration which men of the Renaissance had for antiquity might dispose us to question whether the revolution can have been so complete as some people seem to have imagined—whether, indeed, in respect of this problem in particular, the age of Machiavelli should not be regarded merely as one of transition. And when we consider how much we to-day—the great majority of us—must take our knowledge of the natural sciences, for example, on the authority of others, when we consider how the unexamined verdicts of past historians are even to-day kept in currency by writers of history (so that those who denounce a spirit of uncritical acceptance in the middle ages are in their very decrials sometimes guilty of the thing which they so loudly condemn), we may wonder whether the difference between the medieval and the modern mentality is an absolute one, as people so often tend to think—whether indeed the whole transition from medieval to modern in the region in question is not more banal, less magical and portentous, than it seemed to be at first view. We may note that in any case the overthrow of the authority of the ancients in the realm of natural science for example is not complete and obvious until the seventeenth century. Only in the seventeenth century did the warfare between "the Ancients and the Moderns" reach in various realms of thought its acute and final stage. Even in the eighteenth century Bolingbroke in his *Letters on History* (which have a peculiar relation with the views of Machiavelli) thought it relevant to defend the study of modern times against those who still attached themselves to the ancient world. The significance of the 'experimental method' itself was not fully realized or clearly established until after the emergence in the seventeenth century of new scientific apparatus—the telescope, the microscope, and more accurate measuring-instruments for example; and even Bacon and Descartes, whose names have been so closely associated with the scientific revolution, can hardly be said to have realized the implications of the new method. There is a transition then, but it is slower than many people have imagined and some one has rightly said that the middle ages do not come to an end until the seventeenth century. Machiavelli, as we shall see, has a place in the transition, for in the political and human sciences as well as the natural sciences a change did occur. Machiavelli is interesting not because he is a modern man born out of due time, but because he illustrates one of the mediations by which the transition was to be accomplished.

It is necessary to look at the period that preceded Machiavelli and so to avoid a serious misconception of the mentality of the middle ages. What we are studying—it should be noted—is the blurred twilight region in which mere subservience to Greece and Rome is unconsciously mitigated, and is mingled with gleams of a more modern attitude to the various sciences. A glimpse at the middle ages will show how the bridges to the modern world were being built before Machiavelli's time—how, furthermore, the gulf itself had never been an absolute one as we are sometimes tempted to imagine. It is useful to examine for the moment the case of the natural sciences, a case not irrelevant since it serves to illustrate the intellectual conditions in which we have to take our start; serves also to show that there were analogies to Machiavelli in other fields of thought.

In regard to the constitution of the physical universe the recognized master had long been Aristotle, whose authority was not clearly overthrown until the seventeenth century. But the veneration for Aristotle arose out of respect for the greatest natural philosopher known to have existed hitherto; and it was as difficult to question his system as in later times it was difficult, even for centuries, to question the authority and the system of Sir Isaac Newton. Certainly the middle ages did not revere Aristotle because he was a Christian, and much of his work had come to them though the mediation of the Mohammedan world.

Long before the Renaissance, men in western Europe studied the behaviour of falling bodies, the nature of the material the moon was made of, the composition of a rainbow, the reason why tracts of what was now dry land had apparently once been under the sea. Such problems they would discuss in the light of reason (as the scholastic teachers in fourteenth-century Paris did)—they would not summarily dismiss them by a facile reference to scriptural revelation. And questions like these (it was recognized), were bound to involve observation and experience. They were questions that naturally took their rise from the study and analysis of the concrete world. In the middle ages, in fact, as so often in more recent times, the belief that God or the stars were responsible for an outbreak of plague did not necessarily forbid all study of natural processes that might be involved; any more than the belief that God chastises a nation with war need stop a historical study of the intermediate human agencies which might have provoked a given conflict.

But whether they examined the behaviour of projectiles or discussed the 'plurality of worlds' the medieval schoolmen knew that Aristotle had made more observations on the subject than they had done. Occasionally they accepted Aristotle's observations as most of us would accept any scientist's account of his experiments—without going over the ground again to confirm the matter for themselves. They accepted the view, for example, that an arrow increases in speed after it has lost contact with the bow-string; they accepted Aristotle's conclusion also: namely, that the arrow was propelled by the rush of air.* But until the produc-

*On this point Pierre Duhem in his *Études sur Leonardo de*

tion of the essential scientific instruments that came into vogue in the seventeenth century, there was not the immense addition to the quantity of observed data which we expect continually to find in the annals of more recent science. Since Aristotle, the observation of natural processes with the naked eye had been subject to the law of diminishing returns—since Ptolemy the knowledge of the movements of the heavenly bodies had not been radically transformed, as it came to be after the discovery of the telescope. Too long a chain of inference (by the necessities of the case) would be attached to what we to-day would regard as too limited a range of observations. The sum of the matter was, therefore, that Aristotle's answers to problems that concerned the nature of the physical universe were not only still current at the close of the middle ages; granted all the limiting conditions, we may almost say that they were still as valid as at the time when he put them forward. And we must not imagine that they were always superstitiously adopted even before the Italian Renaissance. Genuine intellectual activity was patently being displayed. The

Vinci (1906), I 128 says: "Aristotelian dynamics bequeathed to the dynamics of the thirteenth century two affirmations which, down to modern times, were considered as being equally incontestable. They were regarded as two laws so based on experiment and supported by observation as not to be open to the slightest doubt. And yet, while the first of these two affirmations embodies a fundamental truth, the second [the one quoted above] represents an error of a very serious character."

medieval schoolman would take account of new data which had been discovered by the Arabian scientists. Occasionally he would contribute an observation he himself had made or a new piece of reasoning that he had devised. If Aristotle had differed from another ancient writer, this would be accepted as an invitation to controversy. And, long before the Renaissance, there had been attacks on Aristotle himself.

One of the most promising features of the Renaissance was the further recovery or the renewed appreciation of systems like the Platonic and the Pythagorean—the emergence of rivals to Aristotelianism among the ancients themselves, the realization that even in antiquity Aristotle's judgements had not been unchallenged. Copernicus, who addressed himself somewhat to Pythagoreans, did not revolutionize astronomy by making more scientific observations; more than once he enumerated the ancient writers who had suggested to him the idea of the rotation of the earth. Above all, we must note that when Aristotle was found to differ from some other ancient writer and this provoked comparison and controversy, the result was often a collation of the observations which the two authors had presented, and a criticism of the inferences that both had drawn from their respective data. So, while yet subservient to antiquity, the men of the Renaissance were impelled—even if perhaps unconsciously— to an empirical method that was to lead to liberty.

It is wrong then. to imagine that the men in the later middle ages (at least) were blind to the importance of observed facts and empirical data. And their subservience to the authority of the ancients was not an unreasoning one—indeed was not unjustified. Furthermore—long before the authority of the ancients was overthrown—we can see how unconsciously men might be drawn, even while intent upon the classical writers; into a more critical analysis of observed data. Discrepancies amongst the Greek authorities themselves (as we have just seen), might seduce the devotee to an independent examination of the evidence; and other examples might be mentioned which illustrate the transitional character of the age—the respect for the ancients combined with the realization of the importance of empirical facts. Some of these examples, we shall see, bring us nearer indeed to the case of Machiavelli himself. Dissection of human bodies was practised in the fourteenth and fifteenth centuries, but in this period, and even later still, it was of limited value; men saw—men only thought to look for—the things which the ancient writers had taught them to expect. When, later in the sixteenth century, Vesalius, the founder of modern anatomy, dissected bodies and made genuine observations for himself, he tells us how difficult it was for him to come to the conclusion that Galen could have made mistakes. It has been shown that in some fifteenth-century medical treatises the author will put forward certain recommendations as the result of his own personal experience; and when these are examined it may transpire that at this very point the author is transcribing a passage from an ancient treatise. (It will be seen later that Machiavelli himself provides an exact analogy with this case.) M. Durkheim, writing on pedagogy in the age of the Renaissance, has told how Rabelais complained against an education which was a training in Words instead of being concerned with actual Things; yet, says M. Durkheim, while telling men to examine Things not Words, Rabelais himself is unable to escape the deficiencies of his age. Certainly he is ready, as he says, to look at Things, but when he does so he always manages to see what some ancient writer has prompted him to see. The example will at least serve to illustrate the transitional character of the Renaissance in regard to the problem that we have in hand.

Finally, there is an example which is simple in character, and presents, though in a different field, the exact parallel to the case of Machiavelli. It is an episode which begins by appearing ludicrously archaic, yet before our very eyes (and somewhat in spite of itself) it undergoes a change and comes to assume a more modern aspect. We are told that in Venice at the opening of the sixteenth century the craft of ship-building was following its accustomed course. It was a family trade, and the man who designed the ships was also the carpenter who helped

to build them. In 1526, however, the government
of the city desired to have a design for boats that
should be suitable for the special problem of
pirates in the Mediterranean; and great sensation
was caused by the ingenuity of a man who Latin-
ized his name as Victor Faustus and was a lecturer
on Greek eloquence. Being a passionate disciple of
the ancient world, and believing that the Greeks
were the masters of all the sciences, he submitted
for the occasion the design for a quinquereme—a
galley on the ancient model, propelled by five rows
of oarsmen. Nothing is more typical of the age than
the fact that Faustus's design stirred up the whole
controversy of the Ancients versus the Moderns;
though, in this case (unlike that of Machiavelli, as
we have seen), the fashion of the time went for a
moment in favour of Faustus, in favour of the absolute imitation of the ancient Greeks. The upshot
of it all was that the government of Venice author-
ized the construction of the quinquereme as an experiment; and—opportunity having been taken to
hold a grand public display—this vessel was put
into competition with a modern one, a galley of the
sixteenth-century type; with the result that, perhaps by a fluke, for the boat never seems to have
done anything later to justify its existence, the quinquereme won—a fact which was celebrated in
eulogistic Latin verses by some of the famous
humanists of the time.

Yet this triumph of archaism had its more significant side—and here we shall find the parallel with Machiavelli most remarkable. Although Victor Faustus had only been moved by his fanaticism for the teaching of the ancient world, he became modern in spite of himself and stumbled unawares upon what we should regard as the beginnings of a more scientific method. Precisely in order to prove that the ancient world had the superiority, he collected all the information that he could about contemporary vessels and about the history of shipbuilding; and he interviewed mariners of all nations when he had the opportunity, comparing shapes of ships and sundry technical details—using the inductive method, but not realizing what he was doing, and moving to a scientific end quite the converse of what he had originally had in mind.

In the light of these examples taken from various fields of thought, it may be useful to find Machiavelli's place in the whole transition that we are studying, and to analyse that appearance of 'modernity' which is sometimes so remarkable in his work. We need not attempt to discuss the actual influence that he exerted, but we may note that the 'modernity' of his tone did not necessarily have decisive effect upon the general movement in the crucial period; the fact that Machiavelli adopted a given method would hardly have commended that method to the sixteenth century. It may be useful, however, to discover to what degree he was merely a mirror of his time and circle, and to what degree his own labours marked a transition to a more scientific point of view.

As we have seen, he was not the first man to make politics the subject of utilitarian inquiry and business-like discussion; and if he has any importance in this connection it is because in exile he accumulated this kind of wisdom into a book. Many an ambassador and official before his time had debated the practical aspects of one policy and another. His own friends in Florence would discuss the political situation with the same grasp of reality, the same absence of medieval abstractions. And Guicciardini, for example, in this respect, was at least as modern as Machiavelli. Books dealing with practical arts, and treating them from a utilitarian point of view were not unknown in that day— works on husbandry and book-keeping for example; and these not befogged by ethical or religious discourse, but purporting to teach only technique, only the methods that would lead to success. Machiavelli, furthermore, is not 'inductive' in the sense that he sets out merely to observe contemporary politics and describe how men actually do conduct affairs. He criticizes the contemporary world without mercy and perpetually tells the statesmen around him how they "ought" to behave; and no one would have resented more than he the suggestion that his maxims were the codification of the practice of the time. If indeed this was the result that he actually achieved we may say that at any rate he never intended it. If he was able to take for granted the existence of the secular state, talking of it, we might say, almost as though it might be a business concern—still his friends and contemporaries in Florence did the same; they were steeped in ancient writers who provided the appropriate outlook and even the terminology required. The 'modernity' that exists on this side is not Machiavelli's and is rather due to the development of the Italian city-states that flourished on large-scale commerce; for here the processes of social change had been speeded up; and the progress of centuries seemed to have been telescoped into a short space. His own contribution really lies elsewhere, as he himself was always so ready to assert. It does not come precisely in the manner he intended; but it is in the realm that he had in mind —in his use of history.

Machiavelli, as we have seen, looked upon history as a storehouse of examples rather than a field of general experience. In his use of historical examples he was inflexible and hard; and in some respects his method was unhistorical. His faults were like those of the seventeenth-century English antiquarians who abstracted precedents from their medieval context and applied them immediately to the conditions of their own day. They were the faults of those forefathers of ours who did not see the

Old Testament as a historical world, but used it as a quarry for texts that were to be abstracted and directly related to the problems of the present time. Guicciardini criticized this use of historical episodes and Bolingbroke in his *Letters on History*—though he too takes history as a storehouse of examples—finds Machiavelli over-rigid on the subject. He prefers rather to say that history is "philosophy teaching by examples," and he will not harden it by restricting its utility to the provision of quasi-technical political maxims. And the rigidity of Machiavelli's method is increased, we must remember, by the fact that for him the Roman example is always the right one.

Sometimes, however, instead of eliciting a maxim from one example, Machiavelli achieves a broad kind of generalization based on a comparison of a succession of instances; as when he shows that the Romans always gave wide discretionary powers to their generals and says that this can be demonstrated in a number of cases. Sometimes he is driven to closer historical analysis because two examples conflict with one another—he is always perplexed when he finds that two contrary lines of policy have proved successful in analogous circumstances at different periods of the past. He asks why this can have happened, for on his rigid view of history the case is somewhat anomalous—it is calculated to embarrass (and it does embarrass) a writer who assumes that from historical examples a correct formula of policy can be deduced. In **Book III**, Chapter 21, of the *Discourses* he shows how "Scipio made himself master of all Spain by his humanity and clemency; Hannibal, on the contrary, pretty nearly effected the same thing in Italy by very different means: that is, by every species of violence, cruelty, rapine, and perfidy." In attempting to explain the matter he concludes that a general has the option of making himself beloved or imposing on men through fear. "It is not very material which of the two said courses a commander takes, provided he is a man of sufficient abilities to correct the inconveniences that may follow from any excess in the pursuit of them." Now it should be carefully noted that here, when he is pressed—that is to say, when on a rare occasion he faces two contradictory examples—he introduces new elements into the discussion of policy; he offers the assertion that success depends rather on the greatness of the general concerned than on the particular option that is made between the alternative policies; and also he introduces a formula of elasticity, almost an element of improvization—for as the choice between the two courses matters little, the important point is the correction of whatever inconveniences may arise from too rigid a pursuit of either. If he had carried these two precepts to their logical conclusion and adopted them consistently, his attitude to political maxims would have been greatly qualified. Indeed, he realizes that he has stumbled against a difficulty and one of his letters gives further evidence of the fact that the contradictory cases of Hannibal and Scipio are a genuine torment to him. He now makes the point that Scipio's policy would not have been so successful if applied in Italy, and Hannibal's methods would not have been suitable in Spain. In other words, when he is driven to further analysis, he reaches a conclusion which—if all its implications are considered—would tend to undermine his system. He discovers a new range of conditioning circumstances that complicate the incident and call for further historical scrutiny. Under compulsion, in fact, he draws nearer to Guicciardini, taking account of the further elements and chances which a given example involves.

This letter, written to Soderini and undated, shows the bewilderment of Machiavelli in the face of a question which to Guicciardini or to a twentieth-century historian would have presented no problem for discussion at all—a question which, however, struck at the roots of a science of statecraft that purported from a given historical example to show that a certain policy was right and its contrary necessarily wrong. Machiavelli declares:

Why it should be that contrary modes of action should both lead to success (or both sometimes to harm) I cannot say, but I should very much like to know. And in order to provoke your opinion, I will be so presumptuous as to tell you what I think about the matter. I believe that as nature has given men varied countenances, so she has endowed them with varied minds and varied dispositions. From this it happens that each man comports himself according to his mind and his fantasy. And since on the other hand the nature of the times may vary and the order of things is not always the same, that man succeeds in his desires *ad votum*, and is happy, whose mode of procedure happens to correspond with the needs of the time; and another man, on the contrary, is unhappy because his mode of action is unsuitable for the times and circumstances. Hence it might well be that two men working on different lines reach the same end because each of the modes of action may be appropriate to its context; and of course there are as many different orders of things as there are provinces and states. But since times and circumstances often change both in particular and in general while men do not change their dispositions or their modes of procedure, it happens that one is fortunate at one time and unfortunate at another time. And, indeed, whoever should be so wise as to know the times and the order of things and should adapt himself to these would always have good fortune . . . But . . . such wise men do not exist.

Under pressure then, Machiavelli can reach elasticity, and can state that good policy is a matter of adaptation to local circumstances; but he can only reach this view for a moment and he admits that he is not satisfied with his attempt to solve the problem which two contradictory examples occasionally present to the historian. There is a chapter of the *Discourses* which asserts "how useful it is to accommodate oneself to the times in order to keep on the right side of fortune"; but again Machiavelli is merely intent on the assertion that a man cannot change his disposition in order to adjust himself to altered circumstances. Again—even when he is face to face with the very question—Machiavelli fails to reach the general conclusion that political tactics in a fluid world must be flexible.

A historian who is wise, however, cannot help transcending his avowed technique. The instances which we have just examined are a confirmation of the point. Machiavelli's method—or indeed any other one that might be used for a purpose such as that which he had in view—was bound to gain its real value from the political experience and the general knowledge of history which the inquirer himself possessed, however little he might be aware that this was the source of any merit that it could claim. Machiavelli was sufficiently acquainted with history to bring very often additional examples to reinforce an instance from Livy. He was sufficiently immersed in the politics of his own day to draw upon a whole range of topical instances. We need not make a mystery of 'the inductive method'—he knew how to examine and collate historical instances. He makes it clear, however, that his aim is the original one—he is using concrete cases to prove that the Romans were politically wise. Recent examples show the errors of contemporaries, for the most part, and he balances them against ancient maxims which he considers to be sound. He sets out to show why Roman methods were good, why ancient maxims proved successful, how a particular stratagem would work. Like Victor Faustus he resorts to an empirical method precisely in order to demonstrate that one can always trust the ancients to be right. So he collates one example with another, examining what we may call the internal mechanism of each. He analyses the way in which consequences proceed out of causes in political life. He throws light on certain tendencies of human nature in politics, certain features of the historical process. His system tends therefore to slide at times into something much more analogous to a modern historical method. It reached perhaps its highest extension in that chapter of the *Discourses* in which he traversed the conspiracies of ancient and modern times, seeking to discover the special dangers which conspirators had to beware of, the precise conditions in which conspiracies were likely to occur or likely to succeed, and the best precautions that a prince might take if he wished to forestall or circumvent intrigues. Similarly his science of statecraft was perhaps most justified—partly by the range of the examples covered, partly by the acuteness of the historical analysis involved—when he criticized Louis XII's invasion of Italy, worked up the subject of foreign conquest from ancient history, balanced modern errors against ancient maxims, and produced the precepts which appear in Chapter III of *The Prince*.

But, though he reached these splendid heights, and though in his works we can trace the steps by which a transition was made from the cult of classical examples to something like a modern use of history, Machiavelli's original principles always remained, and his general theory lagged behind his practice. Above all we must note that sometimes even his practice is not so genuinely scientific as it purports to be. He is an example of what we have already met in the case of the natural sciences—when he observes he sees what the ancients have taught him to see, when he examines the facts he may know beforehand the conclusion that he is going to draw from them. He glances at a historical episode and this reminds him often of some political precept which indeed was already in his mind. At the finish of his examination the truth comes packed and parcelled—it is liable to be a maxim that he has remembered from the ancient world. At the

close of Chapter III of *The Prince*, when he has pointed out some of the mistakes of the French in the
second invasion of Italy, he says:

> From this may be drawn a general rule
> which seldom or rarely fails: that the man who
> enables another to become powerful has
> brought upon himself his own ruin.

Hereupon his commentator, L. A. Burd, remarks:

> It is curious that the general rule . . . should
> be deduced from the consideration of Louis
> XII's conduct; for Machiavelli must have
> known that Aristotle had said just the same in
> a passage which he imitates in detail further
> on.

Even in the chapter *On Conspiracies*, which has been
mentioned, Machiavelli may range over various
periods of history in order to discover his political
maxims; but it is curious that the fruits of so empirical a study should so often appear in the form of
precepts which are translated from Aristotle and
other writers. *The Prince* in particular is an example of what we have already seen in the case of
the natural sciences—for here in the Dedication he
more particularly claims to be giving the result of
experience and in Chapter XIII he says that it is his
desire to restrict his study as far as possible to episodes which are Italian and are recent. Yet as we
have seen, *The Prince* appears to be so modern, be-

cause the debt to the ancient world has on this occasion been for the most part concealed.* Machiavelli believed that human nature was thoroughly wicked, and such a judgement makes us imagine that he was a modern realist. Guicciardini shows that even here he was too doctrinaire—even here he attached himself too rigidly to ancient teaching on the subject. And often his views on the historical process, which have a scientific flavour, are taken similarly from the writers of antiquity.

Very significant, indeed, is Machiavelli's passion for historical analysis—for the study of the foundation of states, the processes they undergo, the causes of their corruption; the study also of the problem of colonies, the conditions under which liberty can be preserved, and the importance of religion for the maintenance of a state—all of which have made some people imagine that the purpose of the *Discourses* was really the scientific examination of the structure and development of states. In reality these things are part of his study of the factors which condition political action; they illustrate further his desire to project a practical ques-

*The classical character of Machiavelli's teaching is illustrated by the curious but pertinent comment made by Mario Praz on the maxims for a tyrant which are found in Act II, Scene ii, of Ben Jonson's *Sejanus*. He writes: "That Meyer, who ignored the Senecan origin of these maxims, could find parallels for them in Machiavelli's writings, shows once more how cautious one must be in the study of Machiavelli's influence upon the stage."

tion on to the larger field of historical survey; but always they issue in some guide to action and this is the avowed object of Machiavelli's work. Even the historical disquisitions in the first book of the *Discourses*, such sections as deal with the origin of states and the most preferable form of government, are intended for the man who seeks to create a state in contemporary Italy; and they lead to maxims for 'Legislators' and new princes who are at the very opening of their work (cf. the example given on p. 54 above). A very modern flavour attends these discussions of what may be called the mechanics of the development of states. Yet in this historical analysis Machiavelli shows little originality and pretends to none; he follows, sometimes he even paraphrases, the work of ancient writers; he is simply a channel for classical influence. Through this he is, however, perhaps the precursor of a modern branch of study; his interest in statecraft does, in one of its by-products, herald a certain kind of political science.

Finally, it would be useless to deny the degree to which Machiavelli succeeded in justifying his historical method—justifying it, not to his political contemporaries perhaps, and not in its entirety, but at least to the student of history and politics in a certain measure. It is no mean thing that Richelieu in his *Political Testament*, should have declared his indebtedness to him. And Napoleon Bonaparte uses points of technique from Machiavelli, and even uses history to a similar purpose. The state-craft of Machiavelli is open to many objections, and these we shall discuss when we come to the examination of the character of the teaching that he had to offer; but there is great prudence and wisdom in much of his advice and often his principles are the result of profound historical analysis. Some of his precepts for new princes give the impression of having been written for a twentieth-century dictator. At the same time he provides many formulas for what we have come to regard as the English mode of conducting politics; as when he says that political revolutions should be concealed by the retention of at least the forms of the ancient institutions; or that it is very offensive to create a new law which looks back too far, in opposition to ancient customs; or that politicians ought to take account of the temper of the times. Some of his maxims entered the English whig tradition—for instance his thesis that a constitution cannot be overturned unless the people themselves have become corrupt; or his view that the mass of the people may be mistaken on general principles but are apt to be right on particular issues; or his doctrine that "where the people are not corrupt, tumults and commotions cannot injure any state; but where they are degenerate the best laws and institutions will be deprived of all their efficacy." However much we may distrust the lessons of history, we must agree that Machiavelli found the way to a method by which great utility can be achieved; the study of all the conspiracies that have taken place in the past may lead to the discovery of quasi-technical political maxims, which are valid, humanly speaking, and are of practical use. And the Marxists have made an interesting extension of Machiavelli when they have gone to history to learn the science of insurrection, the mechanics of subversive activity, and the wider doctrines of revolutionary strategy. The method is dangerous in academic hands, however, and it is only safe when the examination is conducted by a man of assured political experience. To a Napoleon Bonaparte the use of history, which Machiavelli pressed upon practising statesmen, can bring a wealth of wisdom and a multiplication of power.

So we find that the return to the classical world is not a mere return or reduplication, however passionately this may be desired. And history cannot repeat herself even when she tries to do so, and when human agencies are bent upon that very object. Old things may be recovered by antiquarian fervour, but they are recaptured into a new context, and so fresh things are generated, and surprises still emerge. And men who yearn only for ancient wisdom stumble unawares into a wisdom and a world that were unforeseen. That is why the Renaissance is not mere bondage and sterility,

and the study of the classics becomes one of the
gateways to modern times.

One further example may throw light on that
Renaissance world in which Machiavelli finds his
true explanation and his true context. In the clos-
ing decades of the sixteenth century, amongst the
cultured circles in Florence, there was a group of
men who met at the house of Giovanni Bardi, the
Count of Vernio. They included Vincenzo Galilei
—the father of the famous astronomer—who himself provides an illustration of the type of process
which we are examining at the moment. He published a *Dialogo della Musica Antica e Moderni* in
which he defended the art of the ancient world; and
to demonstrate the superiority of this he set part of
Dante's *Inferno* to music for a single voice with lute
accompaniment. Out of antiquarian fervour he
produced a new thing, "the first artistic monody of
which we have any record."

These men, who assembled at the Palazzo
Bardi,

> were enthusiastic students of Greek literature
> . . . It became their fondest ambition to restore
> the Greek drama, but they soon learned that
> in order to do this they must find their way
> back to something like the Greek music used
> in that drama. It was in searching for this that
> they hit upon the much-desired substitute for
> the unsuitable polyphonic chorus. . . It was in

84

the search for Greek recitative that composers found the new thing.

These enthusiasts produced plays on classical themes and set them to music, not merely adding instrumental accompaniment but providing voice parts, the movements of which had sympathetic correspondence with the lilt of human speech; so that they achieved something like an opera which was all recitative, and which—though it might not be pleasing to modern ears—is of the greatest historical importance. In the dedication of the libretto of one of these works, *Eurydice*, the author addresses Catherine de' Medici in the following terms:

> It has been the opinion of many persons, most excellent queen, that the ancient Greeks and Romans sang their tragedies throughout on the stage, but so noble a manner of recitation has not, that I know of, been even attempted by any one till now; and this I thought was owing to the defect of the modern music which is far inferior to the ancient.

We might be reading—in a different realm—the words of Machiavelli; and the statement is confirmed by a declaration made at the same time by the composer of the music of the same 'opera,' *Eurydice*. Writing in the preface, he said that in an earlier work entitled *Daphne*, he had tried "to test the effect of the kind of melody which [he] imagined to have been used by the ancient Greeks and Romans throughout their dramas." At what might reasonably be called a turning-point in the history of this art, the generating impulse is the passion for antiquity.

By 1601 the results of the work of this Florentine circle were being designated as the "Nuove Musiche." These men who sought to revive dramatic recitation and to find a kind of music in which speeches could be declaimed, "had to begin almost from the beginning," says Parry, "and found out the requirements of their art as they went along." Not only modern opera and the use of music for dramatic and lyrical effects, not only the recitative and after that the *Aria* and further developments in musical form, but changes more far-reaching still, resulted from the pivotal experiment which gave a new turn to the history of music. The break with the polyphonic style led to the development of modern melody and modern harmony. Composers found new ways in which to exploit the emotional and technical resources of voice and instruments. This Florentine group represents the Renaissance in the world of music, the break with ecclesiastical tradition and the birth of the modern era. They provide the point at which secularization takes place in the higher reaches of the art, and old conventions are thrown aside. Once again the very passion for antiquity starts men on a road that leads to the undiscovered continent.

III. THE MACHIAVELLISM OF
MACHIAVELLI

THE CHARACTER OF THE STATECRAFT

MACHIAVELLI's science of statecraft claimed to combine the lessons of history, the
wisdom of the ancients, and the examples
of the noble and great. But he did not reckon for the
personal equation and in reality no political teaching has been identified more closely with the single
personality of its author. To-day we regard the
statecraft which he imputed to antiquity as a signal
product of the Renaissance mind. It is a warning to
all who hope to discover the 'lessons of history.'
The mind of the sixteenth-century politician
caught from the past the episodes that were
analogous to those of its own world; valued in
ancient heroes the qualities that would have been
effective in Renaissance Italy; and took from history only the things it could recognize and ratify
and applaud. Much of Machiavelli's teaching,
therefore, is his own, in spite of himself: and we can
regard it in part as the historical product of his
particular world.

Machiavelli was specially interested in what we
to-day might call the pathology of states, the seamy
side of policy, the conduct of government under
emergency conditions. His maxims were very often
addressed to a ruler in the anomalous position of a

Catherine de' Medici, rather than to a ruler in the more established position of a Philip II of Spain. They postulate—and to a historian they reveal—the adventurous character of Renaissance politics. Machiavelli indeed has little to say about normal governments in ordinary happy times. What he does say on a number of occasions is that for these governments no problem really exists. "How easy a matter it is to conduct affairs when the people are not corrupted," he will say in the *Discourses*; and in another place he remarks: "For when people are well governed they neither seek nor welcome any change of government." He instances those Roman emperors "who had no need for either Praetorian bands or a multitude of legions to defend them; because their own goodness and the affection of the senate and the people were a sufficient defence." When he has set out to prove that "if one weak prince should succeed another, it is impossible to maintain any state," he adds, "unless as in the case of France, it is supported by virtue of its ancient laws and fundamental constitutions."

In the second chapter of *The Prince*, Machiavelli tells us:

I say, therefore, that in hereditary states, accustomed to the reigning family, the difficulty of maintaining them is far less than in new monarchies; for it is sufficient not to exceed the ancestral usages and to accommodate oneself to accidental circumstances; so that a prince of this kind, if of ordinary ability, will always be able to maintain his position in a state, unless some very exceptional and overwhelming force deprives him of it; and even if he is thus deprived of it, as soon as the new occupier comes into any kind of difficulty, he will be able to regain it.

A little later he says of the legitimate prince that "unless extraordinary vices make him hated, it is only reasonable for his subjects to be naturally attached to him." And the following chapter opens: "But it is in the new monarchy that difficulties really exist." After a number of chapters dealing specifically with various kinds of new monarchy and the problems that concern these, Machiavelli may give a good deal of advice that can be applied to ancient and established governments; but he is dealing with topics, like the military question, which obviously cannot avoid being of interest to legitimate princes as well as new ones. Even so, he makes a remark at times which implies that it is really the usurper or the 'new monarch' that he has in mind. He will note the fact that what he has to say is applicable to legitimate princes as well as illegitimate. He will point out a procedure that is necessary for old princes and then use the argument *a fortiori* of new ones. He will explain that the Ottoman Empire is not a valid example of a new monarchy, because, though the prince himself may be 'new' and may not have risen to the throne by direct hereditary succession, the rules of the state are old and the people are "ready to receive him as if he were their hereditary lord." When he quotes the example of Ferdinand of Aragon he shows why Ferdinand may for special reasons almost be taken as an example of a 'new' prince. And altogether his advice is directed to the adventurer, the self-made man, governing under emergency conditions, rather than to the traditional monarch, secure in the love of his subjects and sufficiently guided by the ancestral usages of his house. When in Chapter xxiv he refers to all this which has preceded, he expounds what is the real purpose of his book:

> The things which are written above, if they are prudently observed, will make a new prince seem like an hereditary ruler and will render him at once more secure and firm in the state than if he had been established there of old.

Then in his magnificent final chapter, he opens with the question: "Whether at present the time is not propitious in Italy for a new prince." Machiavelli was offering an infallible guide for new princes, who wished to become as safe as old ones. In our age he might have called his book "The Prince: a text-book for usurpers."

The maxims in the *Discourses* do not generally deal with what we should call the problems of normal political life. A large number of them, particularly in the first book, are rules to be observed by the 'Legislator'—the 'new prince,' who is to found a state upon the basis of good laws. Striking sections of the book are concerned with the problems attending various kinds of usurpation or attempted usurpation—the case of the tyrant who wishes to destroy the liberties of a state, that of a general who wishes to overthrow a jealous prince, that of a reformer who wishes to make changes which the people may not welcome, that of the conqueror who intends to enlarge the frontiers of his state, that of the citizen who under the disguise of beneficence and humanity is really aiming at the acquisition of power. There is the chapter already mentioned on Conspiracies. And a surprisingly large section of the book is concerned with questions relating to the art of war.

Machiavelli, then, consciously or unconsciously, exercised an important process of selection in his development of a science of statecraft. What purports to be the wisdom of the ancients is the wisdom which Machiavelli's eye seized upon and his mind chose to take. The political world that might be constructed from his books would closely resemble that of Renaissance Italy. It might be argued that the immense importanc_ which he attached to the art of war, the emphasis which he placed upon the personal military capacity of princes, and the attention which he paid to the military aspect of governmental activity were the result of his admiration and study of republican Rome. These things represented the point at which he regarded his contemporaries as most open to criticism; they represent perhaps the most important lesson which he drew for contemporary rulers from ancient history. It is possible also to say that Machiavelli's interest as a historian and as a student of classical writers on history and politics, led to special preoccupation with the origin of states, the processes they undergo, the crises they have to pass through, and the cataclysms to which they are subject; and this might help to account for the emergency character of so much of his statecraft and that tendency in him to concern himself with issues of a violent nature.

If as a historian he was interested in the foundation of states, and if it was from classical writers that he gained the conception of the rôle which a 'new prince' might fill in Italy, it is true that contemporary conditions would encourage him to turn his attention to this subject. After the French invasion of 1494, it seemed that the equilibrium of the Italian states had been destroyed for ever. Thrones were precarious, every state felt menaced by its neighbour, one ruler might be expected to invoke the foreigner against another, the great states of the peninsula suffered repeated over-

throws of government, and, as Machiavelli re-
marked, subjects were generally ready to see a
change of masters. Italy was therefore familiar
with the problem of the 'new prince' who, under
emergency conditions, attempts to achieve security
of tenure or starts the construction of a new state in
territory recently acquired. It should be remembered at the same time that while he was engaged on
his important political writings, Machiavelli had
his attention directed to certain 'new princes'—or
prospective new princes—of the Medici family.
Concerning one of these he wrote a letter in 1515 to
his friend Vettori, in which he discussed the problems that attended new principalities and spoke
as though he had a special understanding of them.
To another member of that family, Lorenzo, he
dedicated *The Prince*. The new prince could only
maintain himself by a special exercise of skill; if he
had been raised from a private station he would
hardly have the skill "unless he were a man of
great genius"; and if he owed his position not to his
prowess but to fortune or the favour of his family,
then he was "in great danger of losing it unless he
took immediate steps to preserve what fortune had
thrown into his lap." Here is a point at which
statecraft must be something more than pious
commonplaces, old men's proverbs or the moral-
izings of a Louis XIV. The hereditary ruler who
could endure if he followed mere common sense and
routine and who, even if he were wicked, might be

supported by the constitution or the laws—he is quickly dealt with, as though he scarcely needed any statecraft at all. For Machiavelli was interested in politics at the point where we must expect them to be clever and crafty.

If in all this, however, we can say that Machiavelli went to the ancient world with the eyes of the sixteenth century, and carried with him the obsessions he might have gained during the course of his own political career, if in its totality his system of statecraft seems to imply the conditions of Renaissance Italy, this is only the beginning of the problem of the Machiavellism of Machiavelli. He himself has confessed that on one point of morality he differed from his contemporaries, and, as will be seen, that point is precisely the crucial one in the discussion of this question. Guicciardini criticized Machiavelli for his cruelty; showed that in the case of one maxim the very impracticability of his teaching lay in its ruthlessness; and in general charged him with having a preference for what he called extraordinary and violent expedients. And if Machiavelli had done nothing more than applaud the methods of Caesar Borgia, still Guicciardini could argue that Caesar had shocked the consciences of the Italians of that day in a manner which itself would have obstructed the ultimate designs that were imputed to him. Burd has shown how even Machiavelli's friends do not seem to have been enthusiastic in their appreciation of

The Prince; and how from one of the letters of a friend we can gather that opposition to Machiavelli's statecraft existed shortly after 1513, before anything had been published; how also in 1532, which was the year of the first publication of *The Prince*, the book was being interpreted in terms of warning rather than precept. In 1534 the rumour was current in Florence itself that Machiavelli had claimed to have written *The Prince* in order to delude the Medici with counsel that would have ruined them—a rumour which in its very falsity is an index of opinion. It is a question how far even Machiavelli's friend Vettori approved of the statecraft, at any rate in its doubtful features; for he significantly refrained from reply when he was asked if it would be useful to dedicate the book to Lorenzo de' Medici. Machiavelli seems to have reproached even Renaissance despots for a certain over-scrupulousness:

> This is one of the errors which (as I said in my Introduction) the Princes of our times are apt to fall into, when they come to deliberate upon any matter of great importance: for instead of following the example of the ancients on like occasions, they think it is in some cases inhuman and in others impossible to be imitated; which is owing to their pitiful education and their ignorance in the affairs of the world. *Disc. III* 27.

In the political teaching of Machiavelli there is perceptible very frequently a certain flavour which it would not be unjust to impute to a love of stratagem. It can be recognized in the character of some of the maxims, but also in the mode of exposition that is adopted at times. Machiavelli's precepts—even the innocuous ones—often have a suggestion of artifice and ruse, or they are developed in such a way as to savour of cunning; as when he shows a republic that the best way to guard against a rising citizen who is currying too much favour with the populace is not to oppose him openly and directly but to imitate him and outdo him and so to speak anticipate his design; or when the usurper is shown that it is a mistake "to become arrogant and cruel on a sudden without observing any gradation." The maxim "that it is the part of a wise man to seem a fool upon occasion" is not a piece of subtlety recommended to a prince who happens to be ruling in difficult times. It is the title to a chapter which discusses the deportment of a man who intends to overthrow his ruler but is unable to do it yet. The conduct of Junius Brutus is suggested as the pattern to be followed, namely flattering the prince and fawning upon him, "however repugnant this may be to one's personal feelings"; and by this method the would-be regicide may not only ensure his own safety but actually share in the bounty of the prince, and even procure a better opportunity for the accomplishment of his secret design. In another place we are told how imprudent it is, when we are asking for something that we desire, to explain beforehand that when we have got it we mean to make evil use of it.

It is sufficient to say to a man, "pray lend me your sword," without telling him you intend to kill him with it, for when you have got the sword in your hand you may do what you please with it.

Disc. I 44.

In *The Prince* he suggests that a wise ruler might "when he has the chance, foment astutely some enmity so that by suppressing it he will augment his greatness." Elsewhere he says:

In all states, however they may be constituted, there are seldom more than forty or fifty persons that have any commanding share in the administration; and because these are but few in number they may easily be guarded against either by getting rid of them, or by satisfying them with honours and offices.

Disc. I 16.

It cannot be doubted that Machiavelli loved to make such pert discoveries as that a prince or republic should appear to grant out of favour that which in reality they are compelled to concede by necessity; and whereas it is the tendency of books of statecraft—like Richelieu's *Political Testament* or the *Memoirs* that Louis XIV wrote for his son—to contain what so often seem pious commonplaces, prosy practicalities and slow adjustments of means to ends, Machiavelli reached those heights where political maxims have more than the cleverness of paradox, and the swiftness and the niceness of their adjustment to the desired end has itself a sort of poetry and something like an aesthetic thrill. Parallel with his devices for politicians are his stratagems for men of war; as for example, when he explains that in besieging a city you should prevent the inhabitants from feeling that the case is desperate, you should promise them pardon and say you have no designs on them but only wish to restrain some few private individuals among them; and "though these pretences are easily seen through, at any rate by men of sagacity and penetration, yet they generally impose upon the populace, who, since they are desirous of present ease and quietness, close their eyes to the snare which such promises conceal."

Further, Machiavelli did not inculcate the arts of strangling and secret poison, as his enemies seem to have once imagined, but he did set out to prove that a usurper "can never be safe in a State where those are alive whom he has deprived of it"; he did say that "whoever converts a free state into a tyranny and does not cut off such men as Brutus ... will not be able to support himself for long"; he did stress the facility with which conquests could be retained provided the family of the legitimate ruler were extinct; he did teach:

> It is much more dangerous to threaten a man than to put him to death; for in one case a prince exposes himself to a thousand perils, but in the other case he runs no risk at all. When a man is once dead he can no longer think of revenge, and those who are alive will soon forget him.
>
> *Disc. III* 6.

In the third chapter of *The Prince* he says that men must be either caressed or annihilated—"they will revenge themselves for small injuries, but cannot do so for great ones."

The truth is that to Machiavelli there was no profit in being wicked if you did not know how to be downright. The man who was wholly good might be admirable but Machiavelli despised the wicked man who could not be wholly wicked—he taunted him with his squeamishness and argued that he would never achieve the greatest heights. His contemporaries had their tricks and their stratagems but they were not scientific enough. He differed from them in being consistent and in going more consciously to history to learn fresh devices. It is not in his cunning, indeed, but in his demand for greater consistency in cunning, above all in his demand for a more consciously scientific study of method, that he had something to teach even to the princes of Renaissance times. The examples we have been discussing were taken almost entirely from the *Discourses*; they are not covered by any special pleading that may be done on behalf of *The Prince*. They are not covered by what is called the ethics of the state; for Machiavelli sets out to teach not only the tyrant, the usurper, or the good reforming prince, but men who are contemplating the overthrow of a free government, men who are merely preparing to seize a throne. It would be difficult to show any state of society—even the society of Machiavelli's own day—which in real life has applauded that quality in statecraft which was the peculiarity of Machiavelli's own system. The real range of his teaching could not come into anything like consistent operation, such as would show its true character and the lengths to which it can go, save in the life of some usurper who would be extremely self-conscious in his methods and would turn to history for new devices and technical hints. The only true portrait of Machiavellism is a Napoleon Bonaparte. And he is the clearest commentary upon the system.

It is not surprising, then, that a later generation should have taken offence at this Machiavelli who seemed to provide—and indeed did provide—a handbook of ready-made stratagem, that was specially adapted to the purposes of a tyrant. Machiavelli taught a man how to usurp a government, how to perpetuate and increase his power, the methods he must use to take away a people's liberties, and the manner in which he could exercise severities on the population with the least likelihood of ultimate detriment to himself. It is not sufficient to pretend to explain Anti-Machiavellism by alleging that the Reformation and Counter-Reformation produced wilful uncomprehending prejudice—provoked a revival of the religious ordering of society and led to a reaction against the idea of the secular state. It is not sufficient to impute the condemnation of Machiavelli to a distrust of the inductive method, or to a lack of 'relativity.' And since practically all the examples that have been given were taken from the *Discourses* we must not say that Machiavelli suffered at the hands of men who misjudged him because they had merely read *The Prince*. Furthermore it is not true to say that the system of Machiavelli was something less than a science of general statecraft, was merely a drastic remedy for a desperate occasion, an example of the lengths to which Machiavelli's patriotism could go. On the contrary he reiterates that it was the neglect of these arts and rules which had reduced Italy to her distresses in the first place; and it was the whole point of his system and of his general theories of history that the methods of the ancient Romans were permanently applicable and universally valid. The truth is that Machiavelli's attempt to provide a collection of expedients and policies easily led to the provision also of a repertoire of stratagem and ruse. No recondite explanation is needed for those dramatists who brought him on to the stage as a master of all that is crafty—a professional inventor of crooked devices for baffled lovers—and then showed him caught in the very snares he had produced. Orestis Ferrara, in *The Private Correspondence of Machiavelli* (pp. 55-61) has called attention to his self-conscious diplomatic methods when he acted as a match-maker in private life. (See p. 127 below.) Only one twist of the screw—and a touch of spite—were needed to turn him into the preceptor of Barabbas, the source of the miser's sins and ingenuities. And, though it is caricature, it is not meaningless misrepresentation to depict him as a teacher of artifice, holding in his hand a bag of tricks.

MACHIAVELLI'S POLITICAL ETHICS

IT may be said that the discussion of the problems of morality does not concern a handbook
of practical statecraft, a collection of technical
precepts; for the author may be presumed to be
arguing: "If you desire this end it is essential that
you should use this method," and he is not to be
taken as necessarily approving the postulated end,
unless the mere selection of this point for treatment
may be argued to constitute a kind of approval.
Occasionally, Machiavelli provides alternative
courses, and, indifferent to the object that we have
in view, supplies us with a choice of schemes and
methods, according as our purpose may be good or
evil. To a successful general who fears the jealousy
of his prince, he will say that he can avoid disaster
by retiring immediately into private life, volun-
tarily resigning his office before he has been asked
to give it up; otherwise he must straightway work
for the deposition of the prince, must secure the
loyalty of his soldiers, corrupt his officers, and in
some way or other dispose of those whom he cannot
corrupt; must also form alliances and connections,
and win over public opinion by showing that all the
credit for the recent successes is due to himself; and
Machiavelli makes no statement concerning his

opinion upon the ethical question involved, though he seems to regret that few men know how to be either totally good, or, failing that, totally wicked. When he says (*Disc. I* 26) that a new prince who wishes to be absolute must change everything in a state—demolishing the old cities, for example, and transporting the inhabitants to new places—he adds:

> These methods are utterly barbarous and incompatible not merely with Christian society but with any form of civilized life. Every man ought to abhor such practices and choose rather to be a private citizen than reign as a king at the cost of such devastation.

"Nevertheless," he goes on—he is ready to provide a maxim for "the man who does not wish to take the highest path of righteousness." And again he regrets that men are neither perfectly good nor wholly wicked, but prone to a middle course which he describes as *dannosissime*.

Further, it is natural that in dealing with virtues such as generosity, piety, clemency, or frankness, he should evade the ultimate moral question and deal with these qualities as they affect the reputation of the man concerned; particularly as, in keeping with ancient writers, he had large views concerning public reputation and not only produced a wealth of teaching on the subject but also in discussing policy—in discussing for example, the question of remaining neutral when neighbours are at war—showed a remarkable sensitiveness to the effect of a policy on the reputation of the prince. It was natural, therefore, that he should treat generosity, piety, and the like with a certain scientific indifference; strictly speaking it was not his duty to carry these questions into the realm of moral ideas; though at times he does seem perhaps to state his points in a somewhat provocative manner, and there is an irritating trick of quiet understatement, and a disconcerting brevity in some of his remarks.

Machiavelli, however, on a number of occasions does make definite incursions into the sphere of morality, does leave the world of pure technique and assert that certain courses of action are good or are to be applauded; and an example of this is to be found in his references to what may be called the ethics of the state. He does seem to believe that anything may be done if the welfare of the community is in question, that cruelties in a prince may be justified if the ultimate aim is the restoration of order and the safety of society, and that it is justifiable to deceive the enemy with whom you are at war. Too great a significance should not be imputed to these statements, however; nor should their novelty be exaggerated in view of Machiavelli's knowledge of the ancient world. Machiavelli indeed, is inclined to avoid a genuine discussion of the ethical point in question. He seems to be aware that his argument is one not unfamiliar to his contemporaries. What he is apparently concerned with, for the most part, is the effect that certain conduct is likely to have on reputation in a wide sense of the word. When he says that promises extorted by force may be broken he argues that this will not result in any reflection on the honour of the person who breaks them. When he says that any means, however dishonourable, may be used to rescue the state when the state is in danger, he refers to the example of the French people to show that the point is in fact accepted. When he talks of Romulus who killed his brother for the public good, he insists that in such a case *l'effetto . . . sempre le scuserà* and says that no wise man would ever reprove an extraordinary action taken for such a purpose. And if a ruler commits some cruelty or dishonesty for the sake of the public welfare, Machiavelli's argument on occasion is that men *do* forgive him afterwards, posterity *does* approve the act, historians accept it and applaud.

Machiavelli himself, however, said that the interests of the prince seldom coincide with those of the state. One of the three books of the *Discourses* purports to deal with princes only in matters which concern their private interests and not in that part of their conduct in which they could be regaded as representing the state. His maxims were written for princes, usurpers, conspirators, soldiers, and citizens in turn; for princes rather than for states, for princes even when their interests are not those of the state. Machiavelli is willing to tell the tyrant how to move if he wishes to increase his power or to destroy free institutions. At the crucial points his statecraft—in the *Discourses* at any rate—cannot take shelter behind a doctrine which judges conduct by reference to public good.

Professor Powicke has shown how the doctrine of 'necessity' was used to justify the over-riding of positive law as far back as the time of Gregory VII. He has told how Aquinas "argued that in certain circumstances, necessity knows no law; also that a tyrant can be removed on the ground of necessity"; and how the civilians who expounded the cause of the Emperor Frederick II said that "he could not allow himself to be crushed at the expense of the general well-being." Tracing the development through Philip the Fair, Professor Powicke proceeds:

> The next step was to identify the natural law of necessity with the natural impulses of a political community, its rights to natural frontiers and self-assertion, or even to identify necessity not with natural law but with the dictates of history. In their frontier policy, the French kings from Philip the Fair to Louis XIV seem often to be hovering on the edge of assertions of this kind in the course of their elaborate legal arguments and the practice of their elaborate legal devices.

The ethics of the state can similarly be extended not merely to cover the crimes that Catherine de' Medici committed for the purpose of rescuing the country and saving the very existence of central government in France, but to sanction a very different kind of case—the crimes that a Catherine de' Medici may have committed purely to save her own position and power—the crimes that may have had their basis in private cupidity, for example the desire to find ambitious marriage-alliances for her younger children. The maxims of Machiavelli go beyond public welfare in this way and cater for the private purposes of an unscrupulous prince.

Above all, there is Machiavelli's most curious statement on the subject of morality, a thesis which appears in Chapter xv of *The Prince*; and this contains an assertion which, because it is vague, will cover everything. It is more important in that the author points out that in this case in particular his opinion differs from that of his contemporaries. It is the thesis that in the world a man must behave as other people behave; and that if he allows his conduct to be guided by the thought of what men *ought* to do, this will conduce rather to his ruin than to his advantage or preservation. In itself the statement might be meaningless, and on one construction indeed, might be regarded as innocuous. A man can scarcely be accused of any great immorality if he accepts the standards of his time and consents to live as the world lives. The thesis might

prove, however, more pointed and more dangerous if it implied that men should take as their standard of conduct the morality of their day conceived
at its worst; and it is important to note in this respect that Machiavelli had a remarkably low view
of human nature. He does not recommend us to
break a treaty merely when we think that the other
party is going to break it; he says that since men are
wicked the other party may always be presumed to
be about to break it.* And his whole attitude is more

*See *The Prince*, XVIII, where, after saying that a prudent
ruler will not keep faith when it is against his interests to do so,
he proceeds: "And if men were all good, this precept would
not be a proper one; but because they are wicked and would
not keep faith with you, you yourself need not keep it with
them."

Cf. *Disc. I* 3: "Those who have discussed the problems of
civic life demonstrate—and history is full of examples to confirm the fact—that whoever organizes a state and arranges
laws for the government of it must presuppose that all men
are wicked and that they will not fail to show their natural
depravity whenever they have a clear opportunity, though
possibly it may lie concealed for a while."

Guicciardini's note on this latter passage [*Opere Inedite*
(Firenze 1857) Vol. I, pp. 10-11: *Considerazioni sui Discorsi del
Machiavelli*] runs as follows: "It is stated in too absolute a
manner that men never do good except by necessity, and that
whoever establishes a republic ought to postulate that human
beings are all wicked; for there are many who, even when
they are in a position to do evil, choose to do good and the
whole of the human race is not wicked. It is true that in founding a state, and in all other undertakings, one should arrange
things in such a way that whoever wishes to do evil shall be
deprived of the power of accomplishing his desire; not be-

significant if we note that this is a thesis concerning general conduct; it is not conditioned by any reference to the safety or even the welfare of the state. It would have been expressed in different terms if it had meant that everything is allowable which is intended for the public good. Finally it is based on the simple fact that the wicked have prospered and the loyal have been defeated. We may account for the attitude by historical circumstances, we may befog the question with mystical interpretations, but in Machiavelli the doctrine 'live as the world lives' is the ordinary vulgar doctrine that morality does not pay; its only purport is the reduction of the conduct of good men to the

cause all men are wicked all the time, but because it is necessary to provide for the case of those who are ready to do evil. It is necessary to bear in mind in this connection that men are all naturally inclined to the good, and, other things being equal, take more pleasure in good than in evil; and if any man has a contrary disposition he is so opposed to the normal character of men—so at variance with the primary end of nature—that one ought to call him rather a monster than a human being. Each man, then, is naturally inclined to the good; but because our nature is fragile—because in human life at every step we meet with occasions for a departure from the path of goodness—for example through sensuality, ambition, and avarice—the wise, foreseeing the danger, have taken away from men the power to do evil when it has been possible to rob them of it; and when it is not possible to do this completely they adopt another remedy, that is to say, they spur men to righteous action with rewards, or deter them from evil conduct by the threat of punishment."

standards of that of the worst, and it is difficult to see how an invitation to immorality could have been expressed in other terms or placed on a more comprehensive basis. Just as the tendency of Machiavelli's system was to make men more consistent and scientific in their political cunning, so the effect—the very intention—of his remarks on morality was to clear the path for the more general acceptance of the kind of statecraft that he had to teach.

IT has been noted already that though Guicciardini was in some respects not unlike Machiavelli in his theories of history, and indeed expressed the doctrine of historical recurrence in
terms that were very similar, he did, however,
show a greater flexibility in his attitude to history,
and he revealed a truer insight into the nature of
historical change, by holding the thesis much less
rigidly and declining to follow the obvious inferences that could be made from it. Also, though
he himself would not seem to have had a flattering
opinion of his fellow-men, he criticized Machiavelli's lack of flexibility in regard to a further doctrine which in reality was taken from classical
writers—the dogma of the universal wickedness of
human nature. In regard to the lessons of history
and the making of deductions from particular examples, in regard to the whole question of the
mobility of events and the need for improvization
in policy, in regard to the perpetual insistence on
the close imitation of the methods of ancient Rome,
the position of Guicciardini is a criticism of a certain hardness in Machiavelli, who set greater store
upon a book of maxims, who gave his precepts a
more rigid character, and who differed most of all

in subordinating the politician to the historian. It is curious that Guicciardini who was no prude—who in real life was more Machiavellian but more practical and successful than Machiavelli—criticized his severity, toned down some of his precepts, seemed to regard him as trying to be over-clever, thought him rigid in certain points of doctrine and made the charge referred to above, respecting the preference for "extraordinary and violent expedients." It is an interesting combination of criticisms. We might be justified if in the light of this we inquired whether the Machiavellism of Machiavelli was that of court and cabinet or really that of the study.

If we examine now, not the construction of his maxims, but the manner in which he brought them to bear upon certain events and contingencies in contemporary Europe, the view will be confirmed that Machiavelli infused into statecraft a certain quality which we can only call doctrinaire. He has great powers of observation, he has the practical statesman's point of view, but we find in his discussions of policy a curious tendency to deduction, we find sometimes an academic directness in his application of a maxim to a current problem; he stresses historical analogies and is inclined to project a question into the larger sphere of historical survey; and if Villari can claim that his descriptions of foreign states are more profound than the analogous writings of Guicciardini, Machiavelli excels precisely as the analytical historian would be expected to transcend the mere observer. Of Machiavelli's dispatches, indeed, Villari writes:

> We have already noted and shall often have occasion to repeat, that as regards statistics and minute exactitude in the description of special facts, Machiavelli is often surpassed by the Venetian ambassadors, who also occassionally surpass him even in scrutiny of the characters of personages with whom they were in contact and divination of their most secret intentions.

Machiavelli's qualities are illustrated in one of his controversies with Vettori, which turned on the danger to Italy from the Swiss. Machiavelli's argument ran as follows:

> I beg you to consider the course that human events actually take, and the developments that states and especially republics undergo as time proceeds, and you will see that all men are at first contented with self-defence and with freedom from external domination; then they proceed to take the offensive and to gain control of other people. Thus at first it was sufficient for the Swiss to defend themselves from the Dukes of Austria, and this defence won them repute in their own country; then it was sufficient for them to defend themselves from

Duke Charles, and this gained for them a reputation abroad; and later they were content
to hire themselves out, so maintaining their
youth in prime condition for war and obtaining glory into the bargain... Their fame rose
higher and familiarity with several provinces
and many men made them bolder, arousing
an ambitious spirit in them and impelling
them to go to war on their own account...
They have now entered Lombardy under a
pretence of establishing the Duke, but in fact
they are the real rulers there. At their first opportunity they will be lords in every respect,
annihilating the ducal family and all the
nobility of that state; and their next move will
be to over-run the whole of Italy in their own
interests...

I know that to this opinion is opposed a
natural defect of men; first, that they like to
live from day to day; and secondly that they do
not believe that what has never been can ever
be, and they always tend to judge all people
after the same pattern... We must take care
lest [the Swiss] entrench themselves in this
state and begin to taste the sweets of power,
for, if they set themselves to the object, the
whole of Italy will come to ruin.

10 Aug. 1513

Machiavelli's verdict was governed in this case by
his view of the historical development of states, his

conception of human nature, and his admiration for 'armed republics.' He was given to this kind of reasoning, which is perhaps more typical of the historical analyst than the practical politician. Vettori simply replied that he did not believe that the Swiss would "ever be able to do what the Romans had done."

A further example of Machiavelli's reasoning, as it was applied to an actual situation, was his treatment of the question whether England would be likely to remain true to her alliance with France, during a war in which the French were hoping to regain possession of Milan.

The traditional enmity between France and England [he wrote] does not affect my reasoning as it affects many people's; for the subjects follow the royal will, it is not the king who follows that of his subjects. As regards the apprehension which the aggrandizement of the French in Italy may arouse in the English, it must be admitted that this would proceed either from envy or from fear. Envy would come into the question if England had no opportunity for gaining glory on her own account and were left with nothing to do; but since she too can gain glory in Spain we need not count envy as a possible motive any further. As regards fear, you must be aware that a person often acquires lordship without power, and if you will look at the question in the proper light you will recognize that if the King of France gains a province in Italy he does acquire a territory, but in relation to England does not really increase his power; for without the Italian lordship he can invade England with as large an army as if he were in possession of it. . . It is rather France who has reason to be afraid if she comes into possession of this treacherous state. For not only will the Swiss be as ready as ever to make war on her when they are paid to do so, but as soon as they imagine themselves to have been offended by her they will be more determined in their hostility than before. Moreover, it may happen that if France conquers Milan, England will make an alteration in the situation of affairs in Castile, and she may be in a position to do more harm to France from this acquisition than France can do to her as a result of the capture of Milan.

To Vettori [*Dec.* 1514]

Again one can detect doctrine rather than observation; the description of the attitude which a wise student of statecraft might adopt rather than an inquiry concerning the attitude which Henry VIII might be expected to take; and it is not unjust to say that there is something academic in that resolution of the question into an issue of either envy or fear, just as there is something academic in the summary way in which both the envy and the fear are disposed of.

Arguing that the Pope, in this same conjuncture, ought to make an alliance with the French invader, Machiavelli could urge:

You must be aware that the first aim of any prince must be to act in such a way as to avoid hatred or contempt; *fugere in effectu contemptum et odium*. So long as he bears this in mind all will go well with him. This principle must be observed in his relations with allies as well as in his relations with his subjects; and if ever a prince *non fugit saltem contemptum* he is utterly lost.

Now it seems to me that to remain neutral between two powers which are at war, could have no result but to bring oneself into hatred and contempt; for the one power will always take the view that you ought to follow its fortunes for the sake of old friendship or benefits received, and if you fail to do so will conceive hatred against you; while the opposing side will despise you for timidity and irresolution; so that you only acquire the reputation of being a useless friend and a contemptible enemy, and whoever wins will consider that he can offend you as he likes. Livy puts into the mouth of Titus Flaminius the following

words, addressed to the Achaeans when Antio-
chus was persuading them to remain neutral:
*nihil magis alienum vestris rebus est; sine gratia,
sine dignitate praemium victoris eritis . . .*

To Vettori. 20 Dec. 1514

Here is an example of the direct application of a
maxim, based once again upon classical sources, to
an actual problem of the day, a problem upon
which Machiavelli had been asked to give his
advice.

The signs of a certain defect in his contacts with
the practical political situation are seen in a section
of his thought where his greatness is clearly beyond
dispute and his work shows a remarkable largeness
of view—namely in his profound diagnosis of the
condition of the Italy of his day. Villari has shown
how, if Machiavelli was right in theory when he
demanded the creation of an Italian militia,
Guicciardini was right in practice when he said
that such a thing was impossible considering the
circumstances of the time. Machiavelli sighed for
some Italian state that should dominate the peninsula, but this was hardly a practicable thing to
desire at the moment; Guicciardini, on the other
hand, realized that there were Florentines and
Venetians but few Italians, and that men loved it
to be so. Machiavelli's contribution to the saving of
Italy was his conception of the 'new prince,' and of
the kind of ruler that he was envisaging we may say

that he would have had to be born and not made, and that, though he might have been sent from the skies, no system of practical politics could have been based upon the expectation of his coming. Guicciardini, therefore, spoke more to the immediate issue when on one occasion he declared that the only way to keep the foreigners out of Italy was by using diplomatic means to see that they should remain too much occupied with one another elsewhere. When he had to draw up a proposed constitution for Florence, Machiavelli produced a scheme which did credit to his enthusiasm but scarcely to his insight if he expected it to be adopted; it was Guicciardini again who on this occasion kept in view the limits of the practicable. And we must not forget that Machiavelli, for all his interest in military matters and his insight into them, was perhaps too anxious to demonstrate that the introduction of fire-arms did not invalidate the military methods of the Romans. If his discussions of this point reveal in him an awareness of the limited value of such weapons as existed in this period, we may at least say that he was more ready to see present defects than to meditate upon the future potentialities of artillery.*

*Capt. B. H. Liddell Hart has shown in his life of Foch how this man thought that the art of war must be taught by the use of history—that is to say by the method of Machiavelli. Here is a branch of human activity in which (by the necessities of the case) historical study has been a governing in-

In many of these instances Machiavelli was perhaps right in theory, and where he went wrong we might say that it was virtue in him to have gone wrong. He analysed the condition of Italy and of

fluence, and has imposed itself upon a practical art. Perhaps it is for this reason that the common charge against military leaders has been the very criticism that Guicciardini made against Machiavelli's historical method—lack of elasticity, slowness in improvization, a tendency to follow the strategy of the last war when the times demand something new. In the one practical art in which Machiavelli's method has been unavoidable in some degree, we may wonder whether history has not been a stumbling-block as well as a guide; and Machiavelli's doubts on the subject of artillery have been paralleled by more recent examples of conservatism when mechanical devices (tanks for example) are put before the military experts. Villari quotes the opinion of Major Chiala: "After reading the seven books of the 'Arte della Guerra' it is impossible to deny that on everything relating to the unchangeable position of the art Machiavelli writes with . . . lucidity and sense." The word "unchangeable" is not without meaning here, of course; but it implies a point of view that is liable to be dangerously conservative. Liddell Hart notes: The "minute analysis of historical examples became not merely the system applied at the École de Guerre but in all the military educational centres of the world during the generation before the World War . . . The fallacy is the more dangerous because such 'minute study' tends to concentrate the attention on the material conditions—weapons, equipment, transport—of a past case which will be different in the future. . . It becomes clear that Foch undertook his analysis of history not to discover principles, but to illustrate principles which were already in his mind." There is an obvious analogy with Machiavelli here.

Florence as a historian would wish to see it analysed; he urged the adoption of the very policies which
seem right in the long run and in the eyes of history.
It is only when we examine his suggestions as immediate practical propositions that we can complain of them and say that he was perhaps even too
far-seeing. He has affinities with those quasi-
historians of our time who, after making the pro-
foundest analysis of the situation of England or
America, the wisest diagnosis of the European
problems of the day, produce a solution of the difficulties which is only too far-sighted for the ways
of the world, which needs the co-operation of a
large element of fortune if it is to attain the desired
practical result, and which, in too many cases,
demands a very general change of heart in their
fellow-men.

The great policies and systems which he wished
to promote were taken from ancient history or ancient writers; though in each case he retraversed
the field, worked over the internal detail, and examined the various aspects of the proposals. The
rôle and importance which he ascribed to the new
prince, the insistence on a national militia and on
the military aspect of government, the whole
science which he developed for the preservation
and increase of the reputation of the prince, really
represented in him a wisdom that came from the
study of many books. Much wisdom was in them,
and perhaps it would be true to say that no man

completely divorced from practical affairs could ever have elicited so clearly some of the powerful lessons of history. But he reiterates his teachings ineffectually and comes to have the appearance of a man whose mind is burdened with obsessions. Also he had not the strength of character to impose his policies upon the world in which he lived.

The discrepancies of his own political career would perhaps tend to multiply the misgivings one might have concerning his knowledge of what was practicable—knowledge which he not only claimed to possess but claimed particularly to expound in his science of statecraft. It is not easy to judge Machiavelli's success during that active political career, of which his enemies declared that he enjoyed so much through favoritism; and those who have praised his skill seem sometimes to be praising his unquestioned ability as a writer of dispatches rather than his effectiveness in action. Perhaps he was what we may describe as a competent and conscientious civil servant. In his diplomatic work he often failed to secure the object of his mission; and he could miss the object with Caterina Sforza after he had announced success and promised a settlement for the morrow. It is curious that Buonaccorsi considered that he never knew how to get the credit for his own official activities, and on any interpretation the comment is significant in regard to the author of *The Prince*. When some trouble concerning his father affected his own official position in 1509, his friends agreed that the best thing he himself could do would be to keep away from Florence; they would settle the difficulty for him but it was important that he should not come in person. He was for a long period signally unsuccessful in his attempts to gain office after 1512, and that was not because he had been slow in reconciling himself to the victory of the Medici. His attempt to execute a plan for a Florentine militia resulted in complete failure. And we may question the political judgement of a man who imagined that *The Prince* would smooth the path to a political appointment.

There is a further sign of the defective nature of Machiavelli's contacts with the world. It is the disease of a man who can see the shape of things only in the mould that his own mind has made for them—a man who, having glanced at the facts of the case on a given occasion, flies away with the facts, brooding upon them in abstraction, until he has so remodelled them that he cannot remember what his eyes had seen. Machiavelli was one of those people who seem unable to give an accurate account of what they have recently seen or heard—not that we can charge him with deliberate dishonesty, but that his mind became too much the master of what it had once assimilated. In writing his *History of Florence* he could ignore the things which did not shape themselves to the mould he had constructed. On three occasions he gave dif-

ferent accounts of the famous massacre of the mer-
cenary leaders by Caesar Borgia at Sinigaglia. On
each subsequent occasion the narrative was further
elaborated and Caesar Borgia seemed to become
more clever as Machiavelli had more time to re-
flect upon the episode. There is a curious moment
when he attempted to promote a marriage-
alliance between the families of Guicciardini and a
Florentine merchant. In a letter to Guicciardini he
gives an account of a conversation in which he took
part when he was conducting this affair; but it has
been pointed out that the letter has the appearance
of artifice, and it has been noted that in his correspondence Machiavelli—more than his friends—
would indulge in a kind of make-believe, in narra-
tions that are not to be taken at their face value.
His conversation with the Florentine merchant
seems to have been one of those which are turned
into a work of art when they are re-enacted in a
literary medium; and Machiavelli evidently took
pride in the cleverness he had shown, and revealed
a love of the technique of negotiation for its own
sake. It would seem that in this interview he sought
to follow the strategic methods that he favoured in
his official diplomatic work:

His purpose at the start, says Ferrara, is to
inspire confidence; then he desires to create
interest. This achieved, he argues his cause,
giving his reasons, and at the end, if any resis-

tance arises, he sows in the heart of the doubter a vague feeling that he may have to repent his decision. Such was his method when he spoke to the Cardinal of Rouen or to Catherine Sforza; and so it is now when he tries to convince the man with whom, on behalf of his friend, he seeks to make an alliance.

In any case—whatever the technique employed, and whatever authenticity we give to his account of the conversation—the fact remains that Machiavelli was unsuccessful. His adaptation of means to ends seems indeed to have been most cogent when it was done on paper.

The statecraft of Machiavelli, notwithstanding the speculation which it has provoked, has never been brought into real correlation with the personality of the man himself, a personality not without its blighting moods, its moments of bitter irony. If it is considered how very few people, even down to the present day, have been capable of that specialization or dissociation of their interests which would have enabled them to pursue a political problem, as Machiavelli did, irrespective of sentimental considerations—if it is considered how few historians, even, have been able or inclined to consider historical episodes with anything like his calculating mind—it will be felt that there was perhaps a certain abnormality in Machiavelli. The abnormality is, however, reduced, if we hold the view that, in spite of himself, he was a thinker rather than a man of action—he could discuss some topics so callously because of a certain abstraction which is a refinement of the mind; and he could sit and calculate those cruelties which he could never have committed himself. Like Guicciardini in some of his criticisms, we may regard him not entirely as a realist and man of affairs. We may take it that he was a student and writer defective in his contacts with the actual world.

We may not know in what mood of disillusionment or despair Machiavelli wrote on human nature and politics. Works like his might reveal the attempt of a man fundamentally weak to achieve a terrible kind of incisiveness. Perhaps in the very technique of the task which he set before himself there is some explanation of the more unfortunate side of his teaching; a person who studies history with the precise object that Machiavelli had in view will want to see that certain examples of subtlety do not go unexplained and unremembered, but are gathered and polished and stored, to be part of the stock-in-trade of politicians of a later age. Machiavelli loved to expound the tactical point of his maxims, the paradox involved in a piece of stratagem—showing on occasion the snare that would be met if another course, perhaps more obvious and direct, were followed. And at times in the manner in which he states the point one can see a mind that runs to tortuous ways. His style is peculiarly fitted for this purpose; for he writes with an aptness and concentration—a hint of malice sometimes—and he possesses everything that is necessary to prevent him from taking away the spice and flavour of the thing he expounds. A sentence of his may contain the kind of snare which he once claimed for one of his devices. Perhaps he loved stratagem as a bookish man may love it—almost as one might love a piece of dialectic.

This whole study is a comment on Machiavelli's attitude to Caesar Borgia, and something must now be said in regard to his admiration for this man. It should be noted that before Caesar had achieved his great successes, before Machiavelli had come into personal relation with him, the latter in a dispatch of the year 1500, already quoted, reproved Louis XII of France for undertaking conquest without the study of historical precedents, and then proceeded to enumerate the Roman maxims which are discussed in the *Discourses* and in Chapter III of *The Prince*. He had conceived the broad lines of his science of statecraft before he had encountered this pattern of the 'new prince.'

It is a mistake to think that what Machiavelli really applauded in Caesar Borgia was the fact that he showed signs of being a benefactor to his people; though the signs were probably there and Machiavelli would certainly have approved of them. Neither would it be true to say that Machiavelli applauded Caesar for his unscrupulousness, merely delighting in the plain thoroughness of the man. What he loved also was something like the dialectic involved in Caesar's adaptation of means to ends—and the efficacy with which this was achieved in the world of actuality. And even if one might truthfully claim that behind everything Machiavelli admired a mystical efficiency in Caesar Borgia, that was not what he himself stressed, and if we consider his whole attitude to scientific statecraft we should not expect it to be the rationalization that he himself would make. For always he was insisting upon specific points in the conduct of Caesar Borgia that might and ought to be imitated, regarding him as one of those princes of old whose lives contained examples to be followed. The famous chapter on this man in *The Prince* contains the assertion three times over in the space of very few pages:

> For I know of no better precepts to give to a new prince than the example of his actions. . .
>
> I put him forward as an example for imitation to all those who rise to power by good fortune and the arms of others. . .
>
> Whoever needs to gain security in a new principality . . . could find no better example than the actions of this man.

In a letter to Vettori on new princes, dated 1 January 1515, he writes of Caesar that he himself "would always imitate his actions" if he were in the position of a new prince. It is significant that Machiavelli did not insist that Italy could only be saved by a ruler of the genius of Caesar Borgia. He said that any ruler could do it—any prince who followed the maxims he had set down. Such a prince would conquer all Italy and succeed as Philip of Macedon had done.

IV. MACHIAVELLI AND BOLINGBROKE

IT is possible to throw further light upon those aspects of Machiavelli's statecraft which we have been studying—and the man himself can be brought into relation with English history at an important point which has been the subject of misunderstanding—if by way of appendix we turn to the most remarkable of his English disciples, the notorious politician Bolingbroke. It will not be imagined that Bolingbroke himself is our real concern in our consideration of this subject; or that his turgid political writing will bear comparison with the brilliance, the boldness, the subtlety, and the economy of Machiavelli's expositions. What we are studying is an extraordinary example of genuine Machiavellian influence—one which serves to bring out the implications of the man's teaching —serves also to complete the circle of our argument. Bolingbroke himself, therefore, is not the aim of our inquiries and we need only note by way of introduction that it is not the tory politician of Queen Anne's reign whom we have to keep in mind—and not at all the Bolingbroke who at a certain period became entangled with the Jacobites—but the later Bolingbroke who was the enemy of Walpole, the critic of the executive power —an opposition leader who out-whigged the Whigs

—a writer who turned all his scorn upon the doctrine of the divine right of kings, and missed no opportunity for a bitter denunciation of the Jacobites. This Bolingbroke posed not merely as a politician but as a philosopher. And if he was the disciple of Machiavelli, we must remember that he wrote over two centuries later than his master and approached the man from the point of view of English history and of the English mind. He was interested chiefly, therefore, in a certain section of Machiavelli's thought; interested, not merely as a disciple, but also as a hostile critic.

In the *Craftsman* there are many unflattering reflections upon Machiavelli, whose name had long been a synonym for unscrupulousness in politics. In a reference to the freedom of the press in No. 2, we read "Mischievous Politicians are never at a Loss to preserve the *Appearance*, when they have a mind to abolish the *Thing*; a Lesson that was first taught them by their great Master Machiavelli." In the *Remarks on the History of England*, however, Bolingbroke writes:

And though I would not advise you to admit the works of Machiavel into your canon of political writings; yet since in them, as in other apocryphal books, many excellent things are interspersed, let us begin by improving a hint taken from the discourses of the Italian secretary on the first decade of Livy.

Though he seems to be aware that even in the eighteenth century it required temerity to refer to a writer with the reputation of Machiavelli, it would probably be true to say that no author is quoted more often than this one—with and without acknowledgement—in the political writings of Bolingbroke. And even when there is no case of specific borrowing, Machiavelli seems often to be acting somewhat as a magnet to his mind. It should be remembered that Bolingbroke in this period, the period of his actual writings, often affected the tastes and inclinations of the philosopher. If in one aspect we may regard him as a pamphleteer writing in opposition to Walpole, he posed also as a scholar, and *The Patriot King* in particular (as will appear) was written with at least one eye to the judgement of posterity.

The earliest of the *Letters on the Study and Use of History* provide, in one of their aspects, a commentary on the Introduction to Machiavelli's *Discourses*. As usual in Bolingbroke, there is action and reaction, something of imitation and something of resistance, occasionally what almost seems to be a development of the ideas of Machiavelli. Once again we are told not to imitate the mistake of those who go to history merely for the sake of amusement. "The study of history seems to me, of all other, the most proper to train us up in private and publick virtue."

[Yet,] though I attribute a great deal more than many will be ready to allow, to the study of history, I would not willingly even seem to fall into the ridicule of ascribing to it such extravagant effects as several have done.

History, we are told, is "philosophy teaching by examples" and this leads Bolingbroke to a long disquisition upon the importance of examples. "We need but to cast our eyes on the world and we shall daily see the force of example; we need but to turn them inward, and we shall soon discover why example has this force." "Abstract or general propositions, though ever so true, appear obscure or doubtful to us, till they are explained by examples." "When examples are pointed out to us, there is a kind of appeal, with which we are flattered, made to our senses as well as our understanding." "We yield to fact, when we resist speculation." "A habit of recalling [examples] will soon produce a habit of imitating them." Bolingbroke makes the point that historical examples have a peculiar importance, because in them we can see the whole story completed. We can observe a course of events in its full cycle; we are in a position therefore to attach causes to their consequences. In spite of this, he takes particular pains to caution his reader against the mistakes and the rigidity of Machiavelli.

We ought always to keep in mind, that history is philosophy teaching by examples how to conduct ourselves in all the situations of private and publick life; that therefore we must apply ourselves to it in a philosophical spirit and manner; that we must rise from particular to general knowledge. . . Particular examples may be of use sometimes in particular cases; but the application of them is dangerous. It must be done with the utmost circumspection, or it will be seldom done with success. And yet one would think that this was the principal use of the study of history, by what has been written on the subject. I know not whether Machiavel himself is quite free from defect on this account: he seems to carry the use and application of particular examples sometimes too far. Marius and Catulus passed the Alps, met and defeated the Cimbri beyond the frontiers of Italy. Is it safe to conclude from hence, that whenever one people is invaded by another the invaded ought to meet and fight the invaders at a distance from their frontiers? . . . Guicciardin was aware of the danger that might arise from such an application of examples. Peter of Medicis had involved himself in great difficulties, when those wars and calamities began, which Lewis Sforza first drew and entailed on Italy by . . . calling the French into that country. Peter owed his distress to his folly in departing from the general tenour of conduct his father Laurence had held, and hoped to relieve himself by imitating his father's example in one particular instance . . . On this occasion Guicciardin observes, how dangerous it is to govern ourselves by particular examples; since to have the same success, we must have the same prudence, and the same fortune; and since the example must not only answer the case before us in general, but in every minute circumstance.

In order to supply the corrective to Machiavelli, Bolingbroke makes use of a quotation from Boileau which provides him with an analogy.

To translate servilely into modern language an ancient author phrase by phrase, and word by word, is preposterous. . . A good writer . . . will rather imitate than translate, and rather emulate than imitate; he will transfuse the sense and spirit of the original into his own work, and will endeavour to write as the ancient author would have wrote, had he writ in the same language.

This is the manner in which we are to deal with the examples of history—"catch the spirit, if we can, and conform ourselves to the reason of them; but we must not affect to translate servilely into our conduct . . . the conduct of those good and great men, whose images history sets before us." Constantly he repeats the point: "We imitate [these examples] according to the idiom of our own tongue, that is, we substitute often equivalents in lieu of them."

In the second section of these *Letters* (numbers IV to VI) he attacks the view that ancient history is the most suitable for study:

> Such ancient history as I have described is quite unfit . . . to answer the ends that every reasonable man should propose to himself in this study; because such ancient history will never gain sufficient credit with any reasonable man. . . If you take my word, you will throw none of your time away [as I did;] and I shall have the less regret for that which I have mis-spent, if I persuade you to hasten down from the broken traditions of antiquity to the more entire as well as more authentick histories of ages more modern.

When he explains why the end of the fifteenth century is a useful starting-point he shows that he has a sense of the processes of history that goes far beyond that of Machiavelli:

> I say then, that however closely affairs are linked together in the progression of governments, and how much soever events that follow are dependent on those that precede, the whole connexion diminishes to sight as the chain lengthens; till at last it seems to be

broken, and the links that are continued from that point bear no proportion nor any similitude to the former . . . A new situation, different from the former, begets new interests. . . New interests beget new maxims of government and new methods of conduct. These, in their turns, beget new manners, new habits, new customs. The longer this new situation of affairs continues, the more will this difference increase; and although some analogy may remain long between what preceded and what succeeds such a period, yet will this analogy soon become an object of mere curiosity, not of profitable inquiry. Such a period therefore is, in the true sense of the words, an epocha, or an æra, a point of time at which you stop, or from which you reckon forward. . . Should we persist to carry our researches much higher, and to push them even to some other period of the same kind, we should misemploy our time; the causes then laid having spent themselves, the series of effects derived from them being over, and our concern in both consequently at an end. But a new system of causes and effects, that subsists in our time, and whereof our conduct is to be a part, arising at the last period [i.e. the end of the fifteenth century,] and all that passes in our time being dependent on what has passed since that period, or being immediately relative to it, we are extremely concerned to be well-informed about all those passages.

Of Livy he said: "I should be glad to exchange, if it were possible, what we have of this history for what we have not."

In the *Remarks on the History of England* the debt to Machiavelli is more striking and important; and we begin to see how Bolingbroke went to this writer for his structural themes, his fundamental theses in political science. Like the *Discourses on Livy*, this work is a clear attempt to use history for the eliciting of political maxims; though Bolingbroke's views on the nature of history and the use of particular examples differed somewhat—as we have seen—from the ones that are to be found in the *Discourses*. The work is earlier than the writing of the *Letters* which we have just noticed, though for our purposes it is logically posterior; providing, as it does, a practical exemplification of the general principles described above concerning the utility of history. In Letter XVII Bolingbroke again refers to his doctrine concerning "examples," and shows how the story of the Stuart Kings furnishes a case that is now "complete." Causes and consequences, therefore, in this instance can be brought under one view. Many of the maxims come with the flavour of Machiavelli:

> When a prince hath turned the spirit of a nation in his favour he need not be solicitous about gaining particular men; but when he hath turned this spirit against him, he must employ all arts, even the lowest, to detach particular men from the body of the people, and to make them act by motives of private interest against the publick sense.

Sometimes the maxims are those of Machiavelli himself, though occasionally we may find them somewhat qualified; for example:

> A first and essential condition, toward obtaining the love and confidence of a free people, is to be neither feared nor despised by them.

And, writing upon the British constitution, Bolingbroke makes great play with the thesis that the Roman system—the combination of monarchy, aristocracy, and democracy—is the best.

It is in its fundamental thesis, however, that this work on the *History of England* owes its chief debt to Machiavelli. And in spite of the bitterness of the propaganda against Walpole, we must not neglect the academic interest of the treatise—the attempt to organize a collection of principles relating to one aspect of what might be called political science. Almost at the beginning of the work the plan is set out and is discussed with explicit reference to Machiavelli and the history of Rome.

[Machiavelli] observes that, of all governments, those are the best, which by the natural effect of their original constitutions are frequently renewed or drawn back, as he explains his meaning, to their first principles; and that no government can be of long duration, where this does not happen from time to time...

The reason is obvious. There must be some good in the first principles of every government, or it could not subsist at all; much less could it make any progress. But this good degenerates, according to the natural course of things; and governments, like other mixed bodies, tend to dissolution by the changes which are wrought in the several parts, and by the unaptness and disproportion, which result from hence throughout the whole composition.

The most effectual, and indeed the sole method of maintaining their health and prolonging their life, must therefore be to bring them back as near and as frequently as possible, to those principles, upon which their prosperity, strength, and duration were originally founded.

Bolingbroke discusses at some length the decline of the Roman government and the decay of liberty in Rome. He concludes:

The examples which Machiavel cites to show that the virtue of particular men among the Romans did frequently draw that government back to its original principles, are so many proofs that the duration of liberty depends on keeping the spirit of it alive and warm

Now, concerning the fundamental purpose of the whole treatise, Bolingbroke has some explicit declarations in this introductory passage which comprises most of Letter II. It is in connection with the above-mentioned paraphrase of Machiavelli that he deals with the point; Machiavelli indeed has supplied him with his central theme. His intention in these *Remarks on the History of England*, he says, is to illustrate certain "general truths by particular examples." First:

that liberty cannot be preserved long by any people, who do not preserve [the] watchful and jealous spirit of liberty...

Secondly:

That the spirit of liberty, far from [inspiring rashness and undistinguishing fury] is slow to act even against the worst princes and exerts itself in favour of the best with more effect than any other spirit whatsoever.

Thirdly:

that how slowly soever the spirit of liberty may act in suspicious times and against encroaching governors; yet if it be kept alive, it will act effectually sooner or later, though under the greatest disadvantages.

Though the whole work has a topical bearing—it defends the idea of opposition to government on the grounds of corruption in the age of Sir Robert Walpole—it is projected upon a wider canvas, one which provided the central subject of Bolingbroke's political thinking; it is a treatise on one of Machiavelli's important themes—the science of the decay of public spirit, the causes of the decline of liberty in a state, the general problem of degeneracy in the body politic. Bolingbroke slides easily from the technical sense of the word "corruption" (as it was used by opponents of government in the eighteenth century) to the evil of which it was a symptom, corruption in Machiavelli's sense, disease in society and government. He is interested in a somewhat pretentious way in the study of the conditions under which liberty can be maintained.

His maxims are multitudinous: "that liberty cannot be long secure in any country unless a perpetual jealousy watches over it"; "no laws, no orders of government can effectively secure liberty any longer than this spirit prevails and gives them vigour"; "the notion of a perpetual danger to liberty is inseparable from the very notion of government"; "the spirit of liberty exerts itself in favour of good princes; how slow it is to act even against the worst." In the *Dissertation on Parties*, he enlarges still further on the theme, and uses recent history to a purpose that is very similar. "Our liberty cannot be taken away, unless the people are themselves accomplices." "Concessions to the crown from other constituent parts of the legislature are almost alone to be feared. There is no danger that the crown should make them to the others." Sometimes he will quote Machiavelli: "A free government, in order to maintain itself free, hath need, every day, of some new provisions in favour of liberty." Above all he rings the changes on that Machiavellian thesis which we saw condemned in *The Craftsman*—that the most dangerous politicians maintain the forms of liberty, preserving the Appearance, but abolishing the Thing. "The greatest masters of tyranny have judged the form without the spirit of a free government more favourable to their schemes of oppression than all the authority that absolute monarchy can give." "No tyranny can be more severe than that which is exercised by a concert with parliament." "The effects of a bare-faced prerogative are not the most dangerous to liberty, for this reason; because they are open. . . The most dangerous attacks on liberty are those which surprise or undermine." In this connection he is concerned to show that "the corruptions of the best things are the worst."

So Machiavelli provided something of science and something of technique to those enemies of government—whether of Walpole or of George III—who protested against parliamentary corruption in the eighteenth century. He added his contribution to the armoury of those men who cried out that not "prerogative" now, but "influence," was the enemy, and who said that the independence of the House of Commons was being undermined. So—anonymously—Machiavelli even became part of the political heritage of the Whigs; and this—to complete the paradox—through the mediation of none other than the so-called 'tory,' Bolingbroke.

The climax of the influence of Machiavelli, however, comes in the *The Idea of a Patriot King*. Here action and reaction have become greatly intensified, imitation is more direct, and on the other hand opposition is more profound. The book follows the pattern which Machiavelli claims to adopt in the case of *The Prince* and to a certain degree in the case of the *Discourses*; for in all these works the first section discusses the form of the state, showing how the government is acquired and how it ought to be maintained; the second deals with military questions and foreign affairs; while a third section studies the king's attitude to his subjects and friends—the question of private relations within the state.

The genesis of the book, as Bolingbroke explains

twice over—once in the Introduction and then in
the body of the treatise—is due to Machiavelli.
The background lies in Bolingbroke's earlier political writings—in the study of "corruption," the
decline of public spirit in the state. The immediate
occasion is the judgement which might be described as Machiavelli's culminating doctrine on
the subject of the decline of liberty. Bolingbroke
writes:

> Machiavel has treated, in the discourses
> before cited, this question, "whether when the
> people are grown corrupt a free government
> can be maintained if they enjoy it; or establish-
> ed if they enjoy it not?" And upon the whole
> matter he concludes for the difficulty, or
> rather the impossibility, of succeeding in
> either case. . . But, he adds, that "if this can
> possibly be done it must be done by drawing
> the constitution to the monarchical form of
> government. . . That a corrupt people, whom
> law cannot correct, may be restrained and
> corrected by a kingly power."

Now, whether Bolingbroke had a genuine
belief on the subject—product of the bitterness and
disillusionment of a declining day—whether he
merely affected such a belief for a tactical purpose,
or took it as a hypothesis that would give a high
point for an exercise in political science—whatever
explanation we devise for his attitude, we cannot

escape the fact that *The Patriot King* is based on the view that England as a nation had become totally corrupt. A previous essay on *The Spirit of Patriotism* had paved the way for this estimate of the situation. Bolingbroke had found that even his political friends were only too ready to betray the 'patriot' cause. The principles which they had adopted when in opposition, they had been willing to forsake when political power came within their reach. He had reason to be genuine in his sorrow, reason to despair indeed of that 'patriot' party in which he had put his hope. The Introduction to *The Patriot King* purports to pick up the threads that had been dropped in the course of this earlier essay. The "corrupt" are "the greatest part of the present generation," Bolingbroke now declares—probably also the next generation will be in the same condition. In taking this point as his fundamental assumption, he is setting for himself—he is presuming at least for the purpose of an exercise in political science—the problem that Machiavelli had been disposed to regard as insoluble, the situation that seemed to be beyond possible remedy; he is postulating a corruption that has spread throughout the body politic, a degeneracy that has sapped the moral vigour of a whole society.

It seems to me, upon the whole matter, [says Bolingbroke] that to save or redeem a nation, under such circumstances, from perdition, nothing less is necessary than some great, some extraordinary conjuncture of ill fortune, or of good, which may purge, yet as by fire. Distress from abroad, bankruptcy at home, and other circumstances of like nature and tendency, may beget universal confusion. Out of confusion order may arise: but it may be the order of a wicked tyranny, instead of the order of a just monarchy.

Later in the book he says:

To preserve liberty by new laws and schemes of government, while the corruption of a people continues and grows, is absolutely impossible.

The question that Bolingbroke sets before himself has reference to the maintenance of a nation's liberty. The fear that besets him is the fear that a "wicked tyranny" is bound to emerge now that public spirit has utterly fled. Like Machiavelli, he is teased by the strategic problem of the restoration of liberty in a state that has become utterly corrupt. Like Machiavelli he thinks that water cannot rise above its own level, that private cupidities have sprung out of the earth and overwhelmed the public cause. Only a monarch could discipline society again and restore a corrupt people to a knowledge of their own good. Such a monarch, however, with the chance of despotism before him, might choose

—might find it easier also—to use the moment to complete his personal power. It is Machiavelli's problem again—the case of the prince who has both options before him, but the choice lies entirely in his own breast; for society and institutions are presumed to have been disarmed by their own internal decay. The corrupt people are even likely to encourage a king in the very policies that will make their own enslavement final and complete.

It is at this point that Bolingbroke turns on Machiavelli, as though he had diagnosed that here lay the pivotal weakness of his system. *The Patriot King* changes into a violent *Anti-Machiavel*, focusing attention and concentrating its fire at this point of structural defect. The very pattern of the book, as we have seen, is based on the formal scheme followed in *The Prince* and to a certain degree also in the *Discourses*. Innumerable maxims, innumerable vague reminiscences of Machiavelli are embedded in the fabric of the whole work. The unifying thesis, the germinating idea, the motive force of *The Patriot King* are to be found in one of the most daring of Machiavelli's political judgements. Yet, beneath all this, there is hostility—a hostility which indeed is fundamental and clearly avowed. Originally Bolingbroke had given the book a slightly different title—one which showed more clearly the similarity on the one hand, the conflict on the other hand, with the work of Machiavelli. He had called it *The Patriot Prince*, challenging both com-

l

parison and contrast with his great precursor. And in the word Patriot lies the seat of the contrast—the basis of the modification that is to be produced.

> We may be saved, indeed [says Bolingbroke in his Introduction] by means of a very different kind; but these means will not offer themselves, this way of salvation will not be opened to us, without the concurrence, and the influence, of a Patriot King, the most uncommon of all phænomena in the physical or moral world.

In the body of the book Bolingbroke repeats the assertion: "He [the Patriot King], and he alone, can save a country whose ruin is so far advanced." He has no illusions, however, and again he points out that a Patriot King "is himself a sort of standing miracle."

If we catch the over-tones which the eighteenth century supplied to the word, a "Patriot" king would be one who himself took over the programme that had been the property of the opposition—a king who should steal the enemy's thunder, so to speak, and run off with the catch-words of the 'country' party. In the writings of Bolingbroke—more even than in popular usage—the word was loaded also with ethical connotations, which indeed owed something to Machiavelli. "Patriotism" was a synonym for public spirit and a Patriot King must be described as one who (if he is genuine) is moved by a sense of duty. Bolingbroke slides easily from the realm of propaganda to political science and, just as the word "corruption" may have the usual eighteenth-century implications but may move over to the wider meaning that Machiavelli gives to it, so "patriotism"—its converse—is not merely a topical word to him, it is a technical term in a political science that studies the maintenance and decline of public spirit. A Patriot finally, in the eighteenth century, is one who attacks the recognized enemies of public spirit—one who, like Bolingbroke, attacks both the givers and the receivers in the game of political corruption.

A German student (Walter Ludwig: *Lord Bolingbroke und die Aufklärung*, p. 172) has called attention to Bolingbroke's conception of "self-limitation in accordance with the commands of reason." In this connection we may note the passage in *The Patriot King* where God himself is described as a limited monarch:

> God is a monarch, yet not an arbitrary but a limited monarch, limited by the rule which infinite wisdom prescribes to infinite power.

It is important to bear in mind that very early in the Introduction and also in the first sentence of the following essay on *The Patriot King* we have the clue to the purpose of the work. Bolingbroke states explicitly and twice over that he is writing a treatise on "the duties of a king to his country." The first section of the essay—that which in conformity with the Machiavellian model treats of the kind of state that is under consideration—is a veritable hymn in praise of limited monarchy. "Pretensions to a divine right have been generally carried highest by those, who have had the least pretension to the divine favour," he writes, in a bitter attack on that doctrine. "A divine right to govern ill is an absurdity: to assert it, is blasphemy." "Limitations on a crown ought to be carried as far as it is necessary to secure the liberties of the people." "The ultimate end of all governments is the good of the people. . . Now, the greatest good of the people is their liberty." "Every prince who comes to a crown in the course of succession, were he the last of five hundred, comes to it under the same conditions under which the first took it, whether expressed or implied; as well as under those . . . which have since been made by legal authority." All these things are the grounds for a firm opposition to the political teaching of Machiavelli's *Prince*. They confirm the view that Bolingbroke's King is a ruler who consents to be limited—who out of public spirit is even willing to put limitations upon himself. And it is a mistake to imagine that this essay—which, as usual, contains a bitter outburst against the Jacobites—is a quasi-Fascist document, exalting the personal power of the king.

If a state has become corrupt the king can dominate the situation, he is in a position to destroy liberty. This is the datum, this is the very knot that we have to untie—for on this matter Bolingbroke and Machiavelli are agreed. Here—as at the moment of founding a new state—the prince may establish free institutions or may simply prefer to build up a despotism. At the crucial moment everything does depend then upon the genuineness and the sincerity and the public spirit of the prince. "To attain these noble ends the patriotism must be real," says Bolingbroke, "and not in show alone." The Machiavelli whom he chooses to attack, therefore—the one whose system shows a breach at the strategical point—is the one who said that the prince must have the appearance of virtue, the reputation of it in the world, but need not—or ought not—to have the essential quality.

> Machiavel is an author who should have great reputation with persons likely to oppose me. He proposes to princes the amplification of their power, the extent of their dominion, and the subjection of their people, as the sole objects of their policy. He devises and recommends all means that tend to these purposes, without the consideration of any duty owing to God or man, or any regard to the morality or immorality of actions.

In its aspect not as a topical pamphlet but as a treatise on political science, the essay insists that the concept of duty shall be an element in statecraft. Bolingbroke's ethical teaching on self-limitation and his political teaching on public spirit (or the spirit of liberty) now combine, and *The Patriot King* can be regarded in a certain aspect as the culmination of his whole system. Machiavelli in his *Discourses* suggests that a Prince who has attained power by the methods which he has prescribed is little likely to abdicate at the finish and use the power acquired in order to establish free institutions. Bolingbroke says that he will "begin higher" than Machiavelli; and "it is with this [concept of duty] that I shall begin what I intend to offer concerning the system of . . . a Patriot King," keeping "still in my eye the application of the whole to the constitution of Great Britain, even to the present state of our nation, and temper of our people." And Bolingbroke reiterates that a truly Patriot King will always have more power in England than any absolute monarch can possess.*

* Machiavelli, indeed, had made this very point and Bolingbroke seems to admit the fact; but Bolingbroke says that this is not enough. He is anxious to assert that the concept of duty, apart from any self-interest, must actually be introduced into the discussion of political action. Machiavelli, however, in *Disc. I* 10 does seem to go further than Bolingbroke's account of him might suggest to a casual reader. He says that men deserve "nothing but infamy" if they overturn the free institutions of a commonwealth and establish a tyranny. "And in conclusion," he writes, "let those men, to whom heaven has granted the opportunity,

Granted this point, granted a sense of duty and a genuine public spirit in the ruler himself, Bolingbroke can use Machiavelli's own prescription for the restoration of liberty in a state that has become corrupt. Granted that the ethical point is the crucial one, he can apply the Machiavellian thesis that only a king can rescue a degenerate people. We shall see that, utopian though the plan appears—and Bolingbroke admits that a Patriot King is "a sort of standing miracle"—the idea was not without its repercussions in the political history of England in the eighteenth century.

take thought of the two different courses that are open to them; one of which will give them security during their lives and crown their memory with glory at the finish, while the other will only bring them endless disquiet and make them for ever infamous after they are dead." It is true that the concept of duty has not actually been inserted into the discussion. It is true that Machiavelli seems indifferent to the ethical end, since he is prepared to provide so many maxims for the ruler who makes the evil choice. But in the language that he uses and in some of the inducements that he offers to a virtuous prince, he comes very close to the view put forward by Bolingbroke in *The Patriot King*. When he distinguishes between the prince who establishes free institutions and the prince who chooses to inaugurate an hereditary tyranny he strikes straight at Bolingbroke's point. If on the one hand he provides maxims for the tyrannical ruler, on the other hand he is also the real father of the idea of "a Patriot King"; for this latter, re-creating the liberties of a commonwealth that has fallen upon evil days, corresponds with the wise and benevolent "Legislator" of the *Discourses*, who founds a new state and endows it with liberal institutions.

He writes:

> The freedom of a constitution rests on two points. The orders of it are one: so Machiavel calls them, and I know not how to call them more significantly. He means not only the forms and customs, but the different classes and assemblies of men, with different powers and privileges attributed to them [e.g. Parliaments], which are established in the state. The spirit and character of the people are the other. On the mutual conformity and harmony of these the preservation of liberty depends. To take away, or essentially to alter the former, cannot be brought to pass, while the latter remains in original purity and vigour... But these orders of the state may be essentially altered, and serve more effectually to the destruction of liberty, than the taking of them away would serve, if the spirit and character of the people are lost.

Here he is restating a Machiavellian principle which was most apt in its application to the England of the eighteenth century; where the forms of Parliament were carefully preserved but (in the view of Bolingbroke) were nullified by the practice of corruption and the decline of public spirit. Since new laws, new schemes of government, could not save liberty, when a people had become totally corrupt, one could only hope for a king who would bring new vigour to the system "by reinfusing into the minds of men the spirit of [the] constitution."

As soon as corruption ceases to be an expedient of government, and it will cease to be such as soon as a Patriot King is raised to the throne, the panacea is applied; the spirit of the constitution revives of course: and, as fast as it revives, the orders and forms of the constitution are restored to their primitive integrity, and become what they were intended to be, real barriers against arbitrary power, not blinds nor masks under which tyranny may lie concealed.

A Patriot King is simply a king who is possessed by a public spirit; one who, by a voluntary act of self-limitation, though he could create a despotism, chooses to restore liberty. Abandoning corruption, he recovers for Parliament her proper freedom, so that this body once again becomes a "real barrier against arbitrary power."

Will it not be said that this is advising a king to rouse a spirit, which may turn against himself; to reject the sole expedient of governing a limited monarchy with success; to labour to confine, instead of labouring to extend, his power: to patch up an old constitution, which his people are disposed to lay aside, instead of forming a new one more agreeable to them and more advantageous to him: to refuse in short to become an absolute monarch, when every circumstance invites him to it?

Bolingbroke is aware of the objections then, aware that he is asking for a miracle of public spirit; but it is the essence of a Machiavellian thesis that he has expanded—the thesis that when a people has become corrupt, so corrupt that their selfishness and cupidity smother all desire for public freedom, nothing can restore free institutions but the self-abnegation of a monarch who forsakes corruption and rejects the despotism that is within his reach.

When George III came to the throne in 1760 the idea of a Patriot King gained a certain currency; and enemies of the new monarch took to satire and scoffed at the self-imputed puritanism of the new régime. The writer of *A letter addressed to two great men on the prospect of peace* in that year, resurrected the ideas and the very terminology of Bolingbroke —called on ministers themselves "to undertake the work of reviving the constitution," and secure the "Independence of Parliament" by the promotion of laws in favour of freedom of election and laws in prevention of bribery or place-holding in Parliament. Arising from this pamphlet, another, of different authorship, took up the tale, and echoed the demand for a House of Commons that should be able to act independently and issue instructions to ministers. It was entitled: *Reasons why the approaching Treaty of Peace should be debated in Parliament.* Again the ideas of Bolingbroke were retailed. "A fair opportunity now presents itself of restoring Parliaments to their ancient, true, and respectable condition," the author said. Addressing Pitt, who was still in power, he continued:

> The glory, sir, of reviving the practice which Tyranny first suspended and Corruption afterwards effaced, is reserved for you. In a Government constituted like ours, much, almost everything, must depend on the skill and patriot efforts of a Minister.

He was "anxious to restore the dignity and authority of Parliament," instead of having these institutions as "machines moved by secret ministerial springs"—anxious that "our Patriot Sovereign" should genuinely consult with Parliament. Almost as a test case he asked that the forthcoming peace-treaty with France should be debated in a Parliament freed from ministerial control.

It happened, however, that when the Peace of Paris came, the opposition Whigs, under the Duke of Newcastle, chose to make it the first great issue with George III in Parliament; and to meet the influence that they were hoping to bring against the treaty, the king, fighting corruption with corruption, appointed the notorious Henry Fox to conduct the campaign in the House of Commons. It is curious that the issue should have come precisely on the question of that peace-treaty with France, upon which George had been asked to show his quality as a Patriot King; for the tragic personal issue is revealed in a letter, written by George III to the Earl of Bute after the parliamentary victory on the question of the peace-treaty—a letter which has been printed by Professor Namier at the close of his *England in the Age of the American Revolution*. The king writes:

Now I come to the part of my dear friend's letter that gives me the greatest concern, as it overturns all the thoughts that have alone kept up my spirits in these bad times; I own I had flattered myself when Peace was once established that my dear friend would have assisted me in purging out corruption, and in those measures that no man but he that has the Prince's real affection can go through; then when we were both dead our memories would have been respected and esteemed to the end of time[.] Now what shall we be able to say[?] That peace is concluded, and my dear friend becoming a Courtier, for I fear mankind will say so, the Ministry remains composed of the most abandoned men that ever held those offices; thus instead of reformation, the Ministers being vicious this country will grow if possible worse; let me attack the irreligious, the covetous &c. as much as I please, that will be of no effect, for the Ministers being of that stamp, men will with reason think they may advance to the highest pitch of their ambition, through every infamous way that their own black hearts or the rascality of their superiors can point out.

It would appear that George had found himself a prisoner of the system, that a Patriot King would need great weight, at least, before he could release himself from the need of fighting corruption with more corruption. But both George and his enemies would have been surprised to learn the true genesis of the idea of a Patriot King who should restore liberty among a degenerate people—surprised to learn that by the shortest and most direct route possible, the idea had come into English history from Machiavelli himself.

NOTE ON BOOKS

(Works to which incidental reference has been made in the foregoing pages)

pp. 16 Pasquale Villari: *Life and Times of Machiavelli*
etc.   (Eng. transl.).

pp. 22 Francesco Guicciardini: *History of Italy* (Eng.
etc.   transl.); *Opere inedite* (Firenze, 1857), Vol. 1:
Considerazioni intorno ai Discorsi del Machiavelli;
Ricordi Politici e Civili.

p. 53 Georg Ellinger: *Die Antiken Quellen der Staatslehre
Machiavelli's* (Tübingen, 1883).

L. A. Burd: *Il Principe by Niccoló Macchiavelli* (Oxford, 1891).

p. 63 Pierre Duhem: *Études sur Léonardo de Vinci* (Paris, 1906).

p. 67 Emile Durkheim: *L'Évolution pédagogique en France*,
t. II, *De la Renaissance à nos jours* (Paris, 1938).

p. 68 Fred Chaplin Lane: *Venetian Ships and Shipbuilders
of the Renaissance* (Baltimore, 1934).

p. 80n. Mario Praz: *Machiavelli and the Elizabethans* (London 1928).

Edward Meyer: *Machiavelli and the Elizabethan
Drama* (Weimar, 1897).

pp. 84–5 W. J. Henderson: *How Music Developed* (London, 1899), Chapter XVIII.

p. 86 Sir Hubert Parry: *The Oxford History of Music:
Vol. V; The Music of the Seventeenth Century*
(Oxford, 1902).

p. 109 Professor F. M. Powicke: Presidential Address:
Royal Historical Society Transactions, 1936:
Reflections on the Medieval State.

p. 122 B. H. Liddell Hart: *Foch: Man of Orleans* (London, 1931): Appendix: Foch's Theory of War.